World Economic and Financial Surveys

Official Financing for Developing Countries

Prepared by a Staff Team in the Policy Development and Review
Department led by Doris C. Ross and Richard T. Harmsen

International Monetary Fund
Washington, D.C.
2001

©2001 International Monetary Fund

Production: IMF Graphics Section
Cover and Figures: Theodore F. Peters, Jr.
Typesetting: Alicia Etchebarne-Bourdin

ISBN: 1-58906-038-5
ISSN 0258-7440

Price: US$42.00
(US$35.00 to full-time faculty members and
students at universities and colleges)

Please send orders to:
International Monetary Fund, Publication Services
700 19th Street, N.W., Washington, D.C. 20431, U.S.A.
Tel.: (202) 623-7430   Telefax: (202) 623-7201
E-mail: publications@imf.org
Internet: http://www.imf.org

recycled paper

CONTENTS

Appendix Tables

Statistical Tables   87

Bibliography   100

The following symbols have been used throughout this volume:

. . . to indicate that data are not available;

— to indicate that the figure is zero, or that the item does not exist;

– between years or months (for example, 1997–99 or January–June) to indicate the years
or months covered, including the beginning and ending years or months;

/ between years (for example, 1998/99) to indicate a fiscal or financial year;

0 amount greater than zero but decimal points not shown.

"Billion" means a thousand million; "trillion" means a thousand billion.

"Basis points" refer to hundredths of 1 percentage point (for example, 25 basis points are
equivalent to ¼ of 1 percentage point).

"n.a." means not applicable.

Minor discrepancies between constituent figures and totals are due to rounding.

As used in this volume the term "country" does not in all cases refer to a territorial entity that
is a state as understood by international law and practice. As used here, the term also covers
some territorial entities that are not states but for which statistical data are maintained on a
separate and independent basis.

FREQUENTLY USED ABBREVIATIONS

APEC	Asia Pacific Economic Cooperation
AfDB	African Development Bank
AfDF	African Development Fund
AsDB	Asian Development Bank
BIS	Bank for International Settlements
BSSA	UN Task Force on Basic Social Services for All
CCA	Common Country Assessment
CIRR	Commercial Interest Reference Rates
DAC	Development Assistance Committee of the OECD
DDSR	Debt and debt service reduction operations
DRS	Debtor Reporting System of the World Bank
EAI	Enterprise for the Americas Initiative
EBRD	European Bank for Reconstruction and Development
ECA	Export credit agency
ECB	European Central Bank
ECG	Export credits and credit guarantees
EDF	European Development Fund
EFF	Extended Fund Facility
EIB	European Investment Bank
EMS	European Monetary System
EMU	Economic and Monetary Union
ESAF	Enhanced Structural Adjustment Facility
EU	European Union
FSAP	Financial Sector Assessment Program
G-7	Group of Seven industrialized countries
GDP	Gross domestic product
GNP	Gross national product
GRA	General Resources Account of the IMF
HIPC	Heavily indebted poor country
HLM	High Level Meeting
IBRD	International Bank for Reconstruction and Development
IDA	International Development Association
IDB	Inter-American Development Bank
MNSDS	UN Statistical Commission's Minimum National Social Data Set
MYRA	multiyear rescheduling agreement
NPV	net present value
ODA	Official Development Assistance
ODF	Official Development Finance
OECD	Organization for Economic Cooperation and Development
PRD	previously rescheduled debt
PRGF	Poverty Reduction and Growth Facility
PRSP	Poverty Reduction Strategy Paper
SAF	Structural Adjustment Facility
SDR	Special Drawing Rights
UN	United Nations
UNDAF	UN Development Assistance Framework
WTO	World Trade Organization

See also Glossary on pages 75–86

PREFACE

This paper was prepared in the Official Financing Operations Division of the Policy Development and Review (PDR) Department of the International Monetary Fund, under the direction of Doris Ross and Richard Harmsen. Its authors are Christina Daseking, Ulrich Jacoby, Atsushi Masuda, Luis Mendonca, Montfort Mlachila, Robert Powell, Saqib Rizavi, Sukhwinder Singh, Helaway Tadesse, and Nita Thacker. This paper provides information on official financing and the debt situation of developing countries. It updates *Official Financing for Developing Countries* (Boote and others, 1998).

The work benefited from comments by staff in PDR and other departments of the IMF. Opinions expressed, however, are those of the authors and do not necessarily represent the views of the IMF or its Executive Directors. The paper reflects information available when it was issued for information to the Executive Board of the IMF in April 2001.

The authors are grateful to Barbara Dabrowska for research and to Sulochana Kamaldinni and Seetha Milton for secretarial assistance. Jeremy Clift of the External Relations Department edited the manuscript and coordinated production.

This report provides an updated assessment of movements in official financing for developing countries during 1997–99.[1] Financial flows during 1997–99 were significantly affected by the Asian financial crisis, as official financing became increasingly more important in the context of financial rescue packages put together by international financial institutions. For example, net disbursements from multilateral institutions (including the International Monetary Fund) increased from $14 billion in 1996 to $47 billion in 1998, before declining to $6 billion in 1999.

The composition of official financing flows changed, too, as a result of the Asian crisis. Member states of the Development Assistance Committee (DAC)[2] increased official development financing from $73 billion in 1996 to $85 billion in 1999. At the same time, however, new commitments by export credit agencies—a resource not included in the DAC figures—declined during this period, reflecting a slowing down in large-scale projects as governments affected by the Asian financial crisis suspended or postponed a number of public sector projects. For example, new commitments to China, Thailand, and the Philippines declined by 33 percent, 22 percent, and 16 percent, respectively, between 1997 and 1999.

The development assistance effort by DAC member countries, as measured by total official development assistance (ODA) as a percent of donors' GNP, increased slightly from 0.22 percent in 1997 to 0.24 percent in 1999. However, this ratio is still below the 0.3 percent of GNP recorded in the early 1990s—or the United Nations target of 0.7 percent of GNP. It mainly reflects a decline in the development assistance effort of the largest industrialized countries.

Lending by multilaterals during 1997–99 was dominated by lending to the middle-income countries of South East Asia on nonconcessional terms. The IMF lent heavily to these economies to help them deal with the large outflows of private capital.

Several important policy initiatives have been launched since 1997 for the poorest countries. In late 1999, the IMF's concessional lending facility was replaced by the Poverty Reduction and Growth Facility (PRGF) and its objectives were broadened to include an explicit focus on poverty reduction. Poverty Reduction Strategy Papers (PRSPs) are to be prepared by the authorities of low-income countries in broad consultation with civil society and are intended to provide the overall framework for the international community's support to low-income countries. In addition, the Debt Initiative for Heavily Indebted Poor Countries (HIPC Initiative), adopted in 1996, was enhanced in the fall of 1999 to accelerate, broaden, and deepen debt relief for poor countries. The debt relief was more explicitly targeted at financing poverty alleviation. Total assistance committed under the original HIPC framework amounted to $3.5 billion in net present value (NPV) terms with seven countries reaching their decision points[3] and all but one their completion points where assistance

---

[1]For an analysis of earlier developments, see *"Official Financing for Developing Countries,"* February 1998, International Monetary Fund.

[2]The DAC is a committee of the Organization for Economic Cooperation and Development. Members of the DAC are Australia, Austria, Belgium, Canada, Denmark, Finland, France, Germany, Ireland, Italy, Japan, Luxembourg, the Netherlands, New Zealand, Norway, Portugal, Spain, Sweden, Switzerland, the United Kingdom, the United States, and the Commission of the European Communities.

[3]The point at which the Executive Boards of the IMF and World Bank establish the eligibility of a heavily indebted poor country for assistance under the HIPC Initiative.

was released nonconditionally. Under the enhanced HIPC Initiative, by December 2000 total assistance amounting to $20.3 billion in NPV terms was committed to 22 countries (including assistance under the original Initiative). The Paris Club adopted even more concessional rescheduling terms (Cologne terms, with 90 percent reduction of eligible debt) for countries that reach their decision point under the enhanced HIPC Initiative. Many Paris Club creditors have since indicated that they would provide additional debt relief on a bilateral basis, including full cancellation of claims.

The debt relief and its orientation towards poverty reduction is an important contribution to international efforts to help raise the living standards of the poorest in the world. Its success, however, will crucially depend on the willingness of donor countries to increase resources for development aid and link them to the recipient countries' poverty reduction strategies. If debt relief is not truly additional to other forms of aid, it may merely affect the composition and geographical distribution of aid, without leading to a significant increase in total aid flows. It is therefore worrisome that since the adoption of the enhanced HIPC Initiative only a few donor countries have announced increases in their aid budgets that reflect the principle of additionality of debt relief.

NEW OFFICIAL FINANCING FOR DEVELOPING COUNTRIES

Net official development finance (ODF) to aid recipients rebounded in 1998–99, reflecting mainly the rise in financial support to countries that were affected by the Asian crisis of 1997 (Table 2.1 and Figure 2.1).[4] The total level of assistance from DAC member states and multilateral institutions reached $88 billion in 1998 and $85 billion in 1999, up from $75 billion in 1997. Particularly strong was the increase in multilateral non-ODA financing, which reached over $21 billion in 1998 and $19 billion in 1999, compared with about $8 billion in the mid-1990s. This expansion mainly reflected the involvement of the World Bank and other multilateral institutions in the provision of balance of payments support to crisis-stricken countries; it understates the support provided by the IMF as it excludes the IMF's nonconcessional lending.[5] The increase in official lending in 1998 and 1999 reversed somewhat the marked decline in the relative importance of official flows in total resource flows to aid recipients that had characterized the mid-1990s.

In 1999, total ODA provided by DAC countries[6] increased by 8 percent, to $56 billion, from $52 billion in 1998 and $48 billion in 1997 (Table 2.2). The increases in ODA disbursements, however, varied significantly from country to country (Table 2.3). The largest increase of almost 44 percent (or 26 percent in 1998 prices and exchange rates) was recorded by

Japan, reflecting Japan's bilateral support to crisis-stricken countries in East Asia and its contribution to the Asian Development Bank. On the other hand, large declines were recorded by the United Kingdom (12 percent) and Italy (21 percent) because of lower contributions to multilateral institutions.

Total ODA as a percent of donors' GNP in 1999 increased somewhat to 0.24 percent, from 0.22 percent in 1997. However, this marginal increase was not sufficient to offset the sharp declines in the ODA/GNP ratio recorded since the end of the Cold War: in the early 1990s, ODA constituted on average about 0.3 percent of GNP of donor countries. In 1999, only four countries—Denmark, the Netherlands, Norway, and Sweden—met or exceeded the UN development assistance target of 0.7 percent of GNP. During the 1990s, the development assistance effort has declined most markedly in the largest industrial economies, while aid from smaller DAC member countries has remained broadly stable.

The prospects for a sustained recovery in ODA flows and the additionality of debt relief are uncertain. While many DAC members intend to allocate an increasing share of their aid budgets to debt reduction, including in the context of the enhanced HIPC Initiative, only a few countries have indicated that significant increases in their ODA/GNP ratios are planned for the years ahead. Without significant increases

---

[4]This section mostly covers developments during the period 1997–99 as data for 2000 were not available at the time of publication. The analysis of official flows is affected by the systematic differences in the statistics derived from debtor and creditor sources, their coverage of the various instruments, and lags in data availability (Box 2.1). The following information is based primarily on creditor data from the OECD/DAC.

[5]DAC data include only concessional flows from the IMF and thus exclude disbursements from the IMF's General Resources Account (GRA)—the bulk of IMF lending. In 1997 and 1998, use of IMF credit from the GRA by Asian crisis countries on Part I of the DAC's list of aid recipients (Table 2.2), i.e., Indonesia and Thailand, totaled SDR 8.8 billion (rising to SDR 20.8 billion if Korea is included). The multilateral data based on the World Bank Debtor Reporting System used in Section IV include all operations of the IMF.

[6]This comprises direct bilateral flows to developing countries and contributions to multilateral institutions.

Box 2.1. Data Sources and Definitions for Official Financing Flows

The World Bank and the Organization for Economic Cooperation and Development (OECD) are the main compilers of data on official financing flows. World Bank data—published annually in Global Development Finance (formerly the World Debt Tables)—are derived from a debtor-based information system. Disbursements of officially insured credits are classified under banks or suppliers and, as a result, official bilateral support is understated in that it covers only disbursements, not guarantees. The coverage of military debt is not comprehensive.

The World Bank definition of developing countries includes all low-income and middle-income countries (except economies with a population of less than 30,000), including countries in transition. The 2001 Global Development Finance covers 149 developing countries including all those reporting to the World Bank Debtor Reporting System (DRS). Detailed data is provided for 137 of these countries, but aggregate figures also include estimates for 12 developing countries not reporting to the DRS.

OECD Development Assistance Committee (DAC) data—published in the Geographical Distribution of Financial Flows to Aid Recipients 1993/1997 and partly available on the OECD website—are derived from creditor sources. The data are, however, available only with some lag: as

of January 2001, only provisional estimates for aggregate net disbursements were available for 1999.

The OECD disaggregates its aid recipients into developing countries/territories (Part I of the DAC List of Aid Recipients) and countries/territories in transition (Part II of the DAC List). Part II of the DAC List includes most of the countries in transition in Eastern Europe and more advanced developing countries and territories. Several of these more advanced aid recipients such as Bermuda and Israel were transferred from Part I to Part II of the OECD's list in January 1997. The categorization now aligns more closely the OECD's and World Bank's definition of developing countries. Unlike the OECD, the World Bank's classification of developing countries includes most of the countries in transition in Eastern Europe (Bulgaria, the Czech Republic, Hungary, Poland, Romania, and the Slovak Republic) and the Baltic countries, Russia, and some other countries of the former Soviet Union (Belarus, Moldova, and Ukraine).

Official development finance (ODF) to all aid recipients comprises official development assistance (ODA) for Part I countries, official aid (OA) for Part II countries, and other official flows (OOF) for both Part I and Part II countries.

in overall aid budgets, debt relief provided under the enhanced HIPC Initiative may come at the expense of other forms of aid, which would not be consistent with the premise of the Initiative that debt relief be additional to other aid flows, nor with the needs of developing countries.

Distribution of ODA Flows Received by Developing Countries

Bilateral aid allocations were predominantly grants during 1999 (Table 2.4). In 1998 and 1999, 90 percent or more of total bilateral ODA was in the form of grants or grant-like flows (such as debt reduction), continuing the trend

toward a higher degree of concessionality of aid flows witnessed since the early 1990s.

As a result of the increase in financial support for Asian countries, the geographical distribution of total ODA flows changed somewhat during 1997–99 (Table 2.2). Following a decline in aid flows to Asian countries in 1997, the share of the region increased in 1999, to about 34 percent of total flows. This came mostly at the expense of the share of sub-Saharan African countries in total aid flows, which declined by almost 4 percentage points between 1998 and 1999, to 23 percent of the total. This development was also reflected in the distribution of ODA over different categories of countries identified by income level: the share

The OECD defines official development assistance as grants or loans to developing countries on Part I of the DAC List of Aid Recipients that are undertaken by the official sector with promotion of economic development and welfare as the main objective, and are extended on concessional terms (with a grant element of at least 25 percent). The grant element is defined as the difference between the face value of a loan and the present value, calculated at a discount rate of 10 percent, of the debt service payments to be made over the lifetime of the loan, expressed as a percentage of the face value. For example, the grant element is nil if the loan carries an interest rate of 10 percent; it is 100 percent for a grant; and it lies between these two limits for a soft loan. It is widely acknowledged that there are problems associated with the use of a fixed discount rate of 10 percent, as discussed in Annex III of Officially Supported Export Credits: Recent Development and Prospects, World Economic and Financial Surveys (Washington: International Monetary Fund, March 1995).

OA refers to flows that meet the criteria for ODA but are provided to aid recipients on Part II of the DAC List.

OOF comprise flows for development purposes that have too low a grant element to qualify as ODA. The definition of OOF excludes officially supported export credits, since export credits are regarded as primarily trade promoting rather than development oriented. IMF financing from the General Resources Account is excluded, while financing from the Trust Fund, Structural Adjustment Facility (SAF), and Poverty Reduction and Growth Facility (PRGF) is included.

Differences in coverage and definition make World Bank and OECD data difficult to reconcile without detailed knowledge of the respective databases. Part of the explanation for this difference lies in the definition of multilateral institutions and the treatment of grants. For instance, the OECD includes significant grants from UN agencies and the European Union in ODF from multilateral institutions, while the World Bank does not record these flows in the multilateral category. (It uses instead the total OECD grant figure when calculating total flows to all countries.)

Data on officially supported export credits are compiled by the OECD, the OECD and Bank for International Settlements (BIS) together, and the Berne Union, each with different concepts and coverage.

Section II relies primarily on OECD (DAC) data.

of aid flows to the least developed countries, most of which are situated in sub-Saharan Africa, declined in 1999 by almost 3 percentage points, to about 22 percent of the total, while flows to lower-middle-income countries increased in relative terms.

With some exceptions, the distribution of bilateral ODA aid by purpose showed little change through 1999 in comparison with previous years. Almost one-third continued to support social and administrative infrastructure projects, including in the areas of health care and education. Aid flows in the form of emergency assistance became more important in 1998–99, while the relative importance of aid for economic infrastructure and program assistance decreased.

Tied Aid

Following years of steady declines, the share of tied aid (including partially tied aid) in total ODA increased in 1998, to 28 percent, but fell to 16 percent in 1999. The DAC has been discussing a recommendation for a number of years of untying aid to developing countries because studies have shown that goods and services imported under tied aid programs are usually priced above world market prices. However, an agreement on untying aid has remained elusive because of opposition from some major members to a recommendation that did not include a mechanism for sharing the burden of untying aid.

Table 2.1. Total Net Official Financing Flows to Aid Recipients[1]

	1993	1994	1995	1996	1997	1998	1999[2]
	(Billions of U.S. dollars)						
Net Official Development Finance (ODF)[3]	82.4	84.4	87.5	73.5	75.2	88.3	84.9
Net Official Development Assistance (ODA)	55.5	59.6	59.0	55.8	47.7[5]	49.6	51.3
Other Official Flows (OOF)[4]	26.9	24.8	28.5	17.7	27.5[5]	38.7	33.6
Bilateral	56.0	59.0	61.7	48.8	42.3	52.4	53.0
ODA	39.4	41.3	40.6	39.1	32.4[5]	35.1	37.9
OOF[4]	16.6	17.7	21.1	9.7	9.9[5]	17.3	15.1
Multilateral[6]	26.4	25.4	25.8	24.7	32.9	35.9	31.9
ODA	16.1	18.3	18.4	16.7	15.3[5]	14.5	13.4
OOF[4]	10.3	7.1	7.4	8.0	17.6[5]	21.4	18.5
	(Percent of total ODF)						
Bilateral	68.0	69.9	70.5	66.4	56.3	59.4	62.4
ODA	47.8	48.9	46.4	53.2	43.1[5]	39.8	44.6
OOF	20.1	21.0	24.1	13.2	13.2[5]	19.6	17.8
Multilateral	32.0	30.1	29.5	33.6	43.8	40.6	37.6
ODA	19.5	21.7	21.0	22.7	20.3[5]	16.4	15.8
Other	12.5	8.4	8.5	10.9	23.4[5]	24.2	21.8
	(Billions of U.S. dollars)						
Memorandum items							
Net ODF (at constant 1998 prices and exchange rates)	82.9	81.2	76.9	66.9	73.7	88.3	83.3
Total net resource flows[7]	165.7	225.5	265.1	353.7	321.4	230.8	248.0
Net official financing to countries in transition[8]	13.9	14.2	17.8	10.2	12.4	16.6	11.3
of which: Net Official Aid (OA)	6.0	6.9	8.4	5.6	4.1	4.5	4.7
Net ODF as a share of total net flows (percent)	49.7	37.4	33.0	20.8	23.4	38.3	34.2
ODA share of respective ODF (percent)							
Total	67.4	70.6	67.4	75.9	63.4	56.2	60.4
Bilateral	70.4	70.0	65.8	80.1	76.6[5]	67.0	71.5
Multilateral	61.0	72.0	71.3	67.6	46.5	40.4	42.0

Source: OECD.

[1]Data for this table are based on net flows received by developing countries. Tables 2.2 and 2.3 are based on total amounts provided by donors (some of which remain with the multilaterals).

[2]Figures for 1999 are provisional.

[3]See Notes to Figure 2.1 for definitions of ODA and ODF.

[4]Other Official Flows (OOF) include Official Aid (OA)—i.e., flows to countries on Part II of the DAC List of Aid Recipients.

[5]There is a series break in 1997 due to reclassification of some ODA recipients (Part I countries) to OA recipients (Part II countries). ODA figures up to 1996 include the flows to countries that were reclassified as Part II countries in 1997. Differs from bilateral ODA in Table 2.2 because non-DAC industrial donors are included (see memorandum items in Table 2.2).

[6]Includes only concessional flows from the IMF.

[7]Includes ODF, export credits, foreign direct investments, international bank and bond lending, grants by nongovernmental organizations, and other private flows.

[8]Comprises countries in transition on Part II of the OECD's DAC List of Aid recipients. Includes official aid, officially supported export credits and other official financing. Flows within countries in transition are excluded. Receipts reported by some country authorities suggest that the OECD figures may understate the flows.

Aid Policy

A number of important policy initiatives have been taken since 1997 to help the world's poorest countries. In 1999, the international community enhanced the HIPC Initiative, making debt relief broader, deeper, and faster (see Appendix II). In addition, the provision of debt relief was made explicitly conditional on the countries' ef-

forts to combat poverty by establishing a link between debt relief and the adoption of a poverty reduction strategy. In late 1999, the IMF's concessional lending facility was replaced by the Poverty Reduction and Growth Facility (PRGF) and its objectives were broadened to include an explicit focus on poverty reduction. Poverty Reduction Strategy Papers or PRSPs are to be prepared in broad consultation with civil society and will constitute the framework for all concessional lending by the IMF and the World Bank.

The PRSP approach is intended to provide the overall framework for the international community's support to low income countries. It was endorsed by the DAC High Level Meeting (HLM) in May 2000. Donors have a crucial role to play in supporting countries as they develop a poverty reduction strategy. To be successful, a country-owned poverty reduction strategy needs to be supported by all its providers of external assistance. Bilateral donors and multilateral development institutions are expected to contribute to the poverty reduction strategy's design and consultative process, and make up-front commitments in support of its implementation. Given the long-term horizon of poverty reduction strategies, a lengthening of the time period covered by aid commitments would reduce uncertainty on aid flows and the associated complications for policy-making and expenditure planning.[7] The PRSP approach also implies a change in the way donors provide support, namely a reorientation from financing individual projects, that often have overlapping conditionality, to providing coordinated medium-term budgetary assistance.[8]

There are important synergies between the PRSP approach and DAC members' work on implementing their development strategy. The DAC's strategic orientation for development cooperation into the twenty-first century was set out in its *Shaping the 21st Century* report in 1996.[9] This identifies a set of development goals in the areas of economic well-being, social development, and environmental sustainability for 2015, and proposes strategies for attaining these goals

Figure 2.1. Direction of Net Official Flows, 1998/99

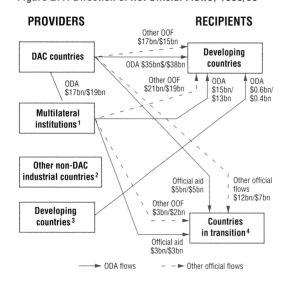

Sources: Table 2.1 and 2.3.

Note: Figures are for 1998/99. ODA: flows of official financing with the main objective of promoting economic development and with a grant element of at least 25 percent (based on a 10 percent discount rate). Other official flows: ODF that does not meet the ODA criteria; includes officially supported export credits.

[1]Multilateral disbursements (including from the IMF) differ from DAC countries' contribution to multilateral institutions.

[2]Flows have been negligible since 1992.

[3]Mostly Arab countries.

[4]Detailed breakdowns of official flows to countries in transition are not yet available. Receipts of official financing reported by some country authorities suggest that the OECD figures may understate the flows.

[7]There is some evidence that the variability and unpredictability of aid have negative effects on growth. See Lensink and Morrisey (1999).

[8]In the IMF staff's consultations with developing countries on the PRSP implementation, country officials have highlighted the importance of donors realigning their procedures and interventions in line with national poverty reduction strategies.

[9]OECD, Development Assistance Committee, 1996: *Shaping the 21st Century: The Contribution of Development Cooperation.*

Table 2.2. Net ODA Disbursements to Developing Countries[1]

	1993	1994	1995	1996	1997	1998	1999[2]
				(Billions of U.S. dollars)			
Total net ODA	56.5	59.2	58.9	55.4	48.3	52.1	56.4
Bilateral ODA	39.4	41.3	40.6	39.1	32.3	35.1	37.9
Contributions to multilateral institutions[3]	17.1	17.9	18.3	16.3	16.0	17.0	18.5
Total net ODA (at 1998 prices and exchange rates)	56.8	56.9	51.8	50.4	47.4	52.1	55.4
Bilateral ODA	39.6	39.7	35.7	35.6	31.7	35.1	37.2
Contributions to multilateral institutions	17.2	17.2	16.1	14.9	15.7	17.0	18.2
				(Percent of donors' GNP)			
Total net ODA	0.30	0.30	0.27	0.25	0.22	0.23	0.2
Bilateral ODA	0.21	0.21	0.19	0.18	0.15	0.16	0.2
Contributions to multilateral institutions	0.09	0.09	0.08	0.07	0.07	0.07	0.1
				(Percent of total)			
Distribution[4]							
Net ODA by income group							
Least developed countries	26.5	26.6	27.7	23.9	26.1	24.1	21.5
Low-income countries	21.9	27.0	25.7	26.1	24.5	26.2	25.9
Lower-middle-income countries	27.4	23.2	21.7	22.6	22.7	22.8	25.9
Upper-middle-income countries	3.6	3.6	3.7	3.1	3.1	3.7	3.1
High income countries	1.6	1.2	1.8	1.4	1.4	1.6	1.4
Unallocated	18.9	18.3	19.4	23.0	22.1	21.6	22.1
Net ODA by region							
Sub-Saharan Africa	30.5	31.0	30.8	28.5	29.5	27.1	23.3
North Africa and Middle East	12.1	13.7	9.9	14.4	11.1	10.3	9.8
Asia	31.0	34.7	31.2	32.8	29.1	31.4	33.7
Western Hemisphere	9.4	9.4	10.8	13.4	11.4	11.1	11.6
Europe[5]	6.0	3.6	3.8	3.8	3.6	3.8	7.1
Other[6]	10.9	7.6	13.5	7.1	15.3	16.3	14.6
				(Billions of U.S. dollars)			
Memorandum items							
Total net ODA to developing countries[7]	56.9	60.6	59.8	56.6	48.3	50.2	51.7
Development Assistance Committee Countries	39.4	41.3	40.6	39.1	32.3	35.1	37.9
Multilateral institutions	16.1	18.3	18.4	16.7	15.3	14.5	13.4
Other flows[8]	1.4	1.0	0.8	0.8	0.7	0.6	0.4
Total net ODA to developing countries as percent of recipient GNP	1.3	1.3	1.1	1.0	0.9	1.0	1.0
Total net ODA to HIPCs	16.4	19.1	19.2	17.1	14.9	14.7	14.4
Total flows within developing countries (net ODA)[9]	1.3	1.0	0.8	0.8	0.6	0.6	0.4

Sources: OECD; and IMF staff estimates.

[1]See footnote 1 in Table 2.1.

[2]Figures for 1999 are provisional.

[3]Includes contributions to the IMF Trust Fund, Interest Subsidy Account, SAF, ESAF, and Administered Account.

[4]Distribution of total net ODA from DAC and other sources, including unspecified. The data reflects the 1996 DAC classification and is thus not consistent with the aggregate data because the country level detail of revised aggregate data is not yet available; however, the revisions to the aggregate data were not large.

[5]Excludes countries in transition not on Part I of the OECD's DAC List of Aid Recipients.

[6]Oceania and unspecified.

[7]Excludes intra-developing country resource flows; based on resource receipts of developing countries, consistent with Table 2.1.

[8]Bilateral ODA from non-DAC donors.

[9]Includes flows from Arab countries and other developing country donors (including China, India, Korea, and Taiwan Province of China).

through, among other things, improved coordination and consistent policies, which are central to the PRSP approach. In May 2000, DAC members agreed to step up their efforts to harmonize donors' procedures.

Donors are taking a more explicit and systematic approach on the issue of ownership and the participation of national authorities and civil societies in the formulation of adjustment programs. Test cases have been used to

Table 2.3. Net ODA Disbursements by Major DAC Countries[1]

	At Current Prices (Billions of U.S. dollars)									At Constant 1998 Prices[4] 1999		Change (Percent)		Donor's GNP 1999
	1990	1991	1992	1993	1994	1995	1996	1997[2]	1998[2]	1999[2,3]	1999	At current prices	At constant 1998 prices[4]	1999
Canada	2.5	2.6	2.5	2.4	2.3	2.1	1.8	2.0	1.7	1.7	1.7	0.5	−1.9	0.28
Denmark	1.2	1.2	1.4	1.3	1.4	1.6	1.8	1.6	1.7	1.7	1.8	1.7	3.2	1.01
France	7.2	7.4	8.3	7.9	8.5	8.4	7.5	6.3	5.7	5.6	5.7	−1.8	2.1	0.39
Germany	6.3	6.9	7.6	7.0	6.8	7.5	7.6	5.9	5.6	5.5	5.7	−1.2	2.2	0.26
Italy	3.4	3.3	4.1	3.0	2.7	1.6	2.4	1.3	2.3	1.8	1.8	−20.7	−18.3	0.15
Japan	9.1	11.0	11.2	11.3	13.2	14.5	9.4	9.4	10.6	15.3	13.4	44.0	26.4	0.35
Netherlands	2.5	2.5	2.8	2.5	2.5	3.2	3.2	2.9	3.0	3.1	3.2	3.0	5.6	0.79
Sweden	2.0	2.1	2.5	1.8	1.8	1.7	2.0	1.7	1.6	1.6	1.7	3.6	7.2	0.70
United Kingdom	2.6	3.2	3.2	2.9	3.2	3.2	3.2	3.4	3.9	3.4	3.3	−12.0	−12.0	0.23
United States	11.4	11.3	11.7	10.1	9.9	7.4	9.4	6.9	8.8	9.1	9.0	4.1	2.6	0.10
G7 donors[5]	40.9	43.8	48.6	44.6	46.6	44.7	41.3	35.1	38.6	42.5	40.6	10.2	6.1	0.21
Other DAC donors[6]	12.0	12.9	14.1	11.9	12.6	14.2	14.2	13.2	13.5	13.9	14.1	2.9	4.2	0.44
Total DAC	53.0	56.7	60.8	56.5	59.2	58.9	55.4	48.3	52.1	56.4	56.7	8.3	5.6	0.24
(in percent of GNP)	0.33	0.33	0.33	0.30	0.30	0.27	0.25	0.22	0.23	0.24	...	...	...	...

Source: OECD.
[1]See footnote 1 in Table 2.1.
[2]Not strictly comparable to earlier data due to the reclassification of some former ODA recipients to Part II of the DAC List of Aid Recipients.
[3]Figures for 1999 are provisional.
[4]At 1998 prices and exchange rates.
[5]Excludes debt forgiveness of non-ODA claims.
[6]Includes Australia, Austria, Belgium, Finland, Ireland, Luxembourg, New Zealand, Norway, Portugal, Spain, and Switzerland.

Table 2.4. Composition of Bilateral Net ODA Disbursements to Developing Countries

	1993	1994	1995	1996	1997	1998	1999[1]
				(Billions of U.S. dollars)			
Total Net ODA	56.5	59.2	58.9	55.4	48.3	52.1	56.4
Bilateral ODA	39.4	41.3	40.6	39.1	32.3	35.1	37.9
Contributions to multilateral institutions[1]	17.1	17.9	18.3	16.3	16.0	17.0	18.5
Composition of bilateral net ODA							
By type of assistance							
Grants	33.4	35.2	36.2	36.5	31.2	32.4	33.9
of which							
Project grants	. . .	. . .	3.2	3.0	3.6	3.6	2.9
Program grants	. . .	. . .	1.9	2.2	1.8	3.1	3.8
Technical cooperation	13.0	12.8	14.3	14.1	12.9	13.0	13.0
Food aid	1.7	1.8	1.3	0.8	1.1	0.9	1.0
Emergency relief	3.3	3.5	3.1	2.7	2.2	2.8	4.4
Debt forgiveness	2.7	3.5	3.7	3.4	3.1	3.0	2.3
Non-Grants	5.9	6.1	4.4	2.6	1.1	2.7	4.0
				(Percent)			
By Purpose of Aid[2]							
Social and administrative infrastructure	25.1	27.3	30.5	30.0	29.2	30.4	29.9
of which							
Education	9.5	10.7	11.2	10.8	11.2	10.6	10.7
Health and population	4.1	4.9	5.6	6.0	4.9	5.5	6.0
Economic infrastructure	19.3	21.2	23.7	23.1	23.4	17.7	17.2
Production	13.2	11.0	10.6	13.1	10.7	9.5	8.1
Multisector	4.1	3.9	5.0	5.8	7.7	7.2	7.4
Program assistance	9.7	4.9	5.8	4.7	4.1	8.4	6.9
Debt relief[3]	10.2	11.5	7.3	5.7	8.8	8.6	7.4
Emergency aid	6.1	4.5	5.2	5.1	4.7	6.2	11.1
Administrative expenses	3.3	4.5	4.8	5.0	5.7	5.9	5.9
Unspecified	9.0	11.2	7.1	7.5	5.7	6.1	6.1
				(Percent)			
By tying status[4]							
Untied	55.5	65.8	77.7	70.2	83.2	72.2	83.8
Partially untied	8.7	3.3	4.6	3.1	3.0	4.6	4.7
Tied	35.8	30.8	17.7	26.7	13.8	23.2	11.5

Source: OECD.
[1]Provisional.
[2]Including forgiveness of non-ODA debt.
[3]Based on commitments.
[4]Based on commitments of bilateral ODA (excludes technical cooperation and adminstrative costs).

develop specific proposals to enhance owner-ship. Wide consultations with developing coun-tries led to the 1998 working checklist of ac-tions to advance ownership and harmonize donor procedures.[10] Nevertheless, there have been concerns among some DAC members over the speed with which DAC principles have been put into practice. At their May 1999 High Level Meeting, DAC members set out a number of concrete measures by which they and multi-lateral agencies could further tangibly improve co-ordination. These included: supporting country capacity to set the recipients' own strategies and aid coordination; linking aid to improvements in aid effectiveness; promoting regional approaches to development; reducing the proliferation of projects and harmonizing donor procedures; doing more monitoring and

[10]*Strengthening Development Partnerships: A Working Checklist,* OECD, April 1998.

evaluation on a joint basis; and facilitating participation by civil society in efforts to improve the efficiency of aid processes. The DAC's work on aid effectiveness has focused on peer reviews and strengthening aid evaluation efforts.

Recent work on aid effectiveness by the World Bank,[11] based on new empirical evidence, points to important conclusions for aid policy.

- *First*, financial aid works better where countries have good economic management (as measured by macroeconomic stability, effectiveness of the legal system, competence of the bureaucracy, and absence of corruption) and contributes to higher per capita growth rates.

- *Second*, where there is a willingness to reform combined with national ownership of reform efforts, aid—in the form of ideas, training and finance—can provide critical support. Experience shows, however, that financial aid can be counterproductive and delay adjustment where there is limited interest in reform, and in these circumstances ideas, or the knowledge creation side of aid, can work better than financing to generate reforms. Indeed, the evaluation of development aid should focus in part on the extent to which development agencies have used their resources to stimulate the policy reforms and institutional changes that lead to better outcomes.

- *Third*, in a good policy environment aid complements and helps attract private investment through increased confidence in policy sustainability and reduced perceptions of risk, whereas in countries with poor management aid displaces private investment.

- *Fourth*, aid is fungible[12] and, in general, project finance does not increase spending in any sector more than an untied grant. Aid is financing the entire public sector and it is the overall quality of policies and institutions that is key to securing high returns on aid.

- *Fifth*, the approach to project design and service delivery that includes the active participation of civil society can result in major improvements. Many projects have supported this approach in recent years.

Current aid allocations could be improved and have a higher impact on poverty reduction. Recent World Bank research[13] shows that aid is primarily allocated as an inducement to policy reform and, as a result, is targeted to weak policy environments. A more efficient allocation of aid could substantially increase the number of people lifted out of absolute poverty. In such an efficient allocation, aid would be tapered in with policy reform, rather than withdrawn as reforms progress.

A working set of core development indicators has been developed to monitor progress in implementing the 2015 development goals (Appendix V). Impetus to this effort was provided by the adoption in 1998 by the OECD, World Bank, and UN, in cooperation with developing countries and bilateral donors, of a working set of core development indicators. While these indicators currently exist alongside other sets of social indicators used by the UN, the aim is to arrive at a universally shared set. Systematic monitoring of implementation is crucial to the success of the PRSP approach. Improvements in the availability and quality of data on social indicators are an urgent priority.[14] In addition, further work is required to refine environmental in-

---

[11]World Bank, *Assessing Aid: What Works, What Doesn't, and Why,* November 1998.

[12]See Feyzioglu, Swaroop, and Zhu (1998).

[13]See Collier and Dollar (1999).

[14]Agreement was reached in November 1999 to launch a shared international strategy to ensure adequate funding and support for national statistical systems—Partnerships in Statistics for Development in the 21st Century (PARIS-21). The objective is to bring all development partners together to make a real difference in providing statistics for evidence-based policymaking.

dicators and to identify indicators of participation and good governance.

The DAC and OECD have also launched a three-year work program on sustainable development, focusing on climate change, technological cooperation, and environmental sustainability. On trade and investment, the DAC is collaborating with the World Trade Organization (WTO) and other multilateral organizations that are supporting an initiative to increase trade opportunities and capacities of the least developed countries. A report on the links between trade, investment, and development was discussed by the HLM and OECD

ministerial council in May 1999, and among its conclusions was a recommendation that OECD countries need to ensure greater policy coherence.

The G-7 leaders reconfirmed their support for the DAC strategy. At the Cologne Summit in June 1999, G-7 leaders noted their commitment to a real and effective partnership with poorer developing countries to reach the economic and social development goals set out in the DAC Strategy. Their commitment to strengthening the effectiveness of ODA in support of countries' own efforts to tackle poverty was confirmed at the Okinawa Summit in July 2000.

RECENT DEVELOPMENTS IN EXPORT CREDITS

Officially supported export credits represent a large share of the external debt of developing countries and economies in transition. In 1999, they accounted for more than 19 percent of the total indebtedness of these countries and for almost half of their indebtedness to official creditors.[15] In addition, exports covered by Berne Union members—largely through new export credit insurance and guarantees, but also through some direct lending—accounted for about 9 percent of all exports from Berne Union member countries.

Total Export Credit

As a result of the impact of the Asian financial crisis, export credit exposure to developing countries and economies in transition resumed its longer-term declining trend in 1999, following a modest increase in the previous year (Figure 3.1).[16] Approximately two-thirds of the total exposure of export credit agencies (ECAs) represented outstanding commitments[17] both in short-term and medium- and long-term export credits, while unrecovered claims and arrears accounted for the remaining one-third. While short-term exposure remained virtually unchanged during 1997–99, medium- and long-term exposure declined, reflecting the slowdown in large-scale projects in emerging markets. Unrecovered claims and arrears varied during

1997–99 in line with the ups and downs in payments on insurance claims by agencies in the context of Paris Club debt rescheduling.

ECAs' exposure remained concentrated in relatively few countries. The 20 main recipients accounted for over 80 percent of agencies' total exposure (Figure 3.2). Agencies' exposure to Russia and China exceeded by far that to other countries, accounting for about 13 percent and 11 percent, respectively, of their total portfolio. In 1999, agencies' exposure to Russia[18] decreased by 13 percent, to $56 billion, reflecting in part repayments on rescheduled loans and limited new business; exposure to China decreased by 12 percent to $46 billion,[19] reflecting the recent decline in major capital investments.

The steady decline in total new export credit commitments to developing countries and economies in transition since 1995 accelerated in 1998–99 in the wake of the Asian crisis. In particular, new commitments reported to the Berne Union fell sharply by 20 percent in 1998 and by 16 percent in 1999 to about $67 billion, reflecting substantial declines in most major markets (Figures 3.3 and 3.4). In general, recent trends in new commitments represent a slowing in large-scale projects in Asia. Governments in countries affected by the Asian crisis suspended a number of new projects in the public sector, which tend to be lumpy, and private investment has slowed down with exchange rate depreciations often eroding the economic viability

---

[15]For a discussion of the role of export credit agencies in financing developing countries and economies in transition, and of the basic features of official support for export credits, see Stephens (1999).

[16]Specific figures need to be interpreted with caution. Starting in 1994, the figures supplied by the Berne Union include data for some smaller export credit agencies, and cover 20 additional debtor countries. The effect of this coverage expansion was reflected in total exposure in 1994 and on new commitments in 1995. For problems that arise in discussions of export credit statistics, see Kuhn, Horvath, and Jarvis (1995).

[17]These include undisbursed commitments, so actual outstanding credit is lower.

[18]Claims on the former Soviet Union assumed by Russia reflected 60 percent of this.

[19]In addition, agency exposure to the Hong Kong Special Administrative Region (SAR) was $7 billion, or just over 2 percent of ECAs' total portfolio.

of projects with little direct foreign exchange earnings.

By the end of 1999, export credits accounted, on average, for about 27 percent of the total external debt of the largest recipients of export credits (Figure 3.5). For several oil producing countries (Nigeria, Algeria, Iran, Oman) or countries in transition (Uzbekistan, Turkmenistan, Azerbaijan), export credits represented half or more of their external debt, in some cases representing long-standing debt or arrears rather than recent export credit financing. For other countries with a more diversified base of foreign financing, such as major Latin American and Asian countries, export credits represented less than 20 percent of their external debt.

Financial Performance of Export Credit Agencies

The financial performance of most export credit agencies, as measured by net cash flow, improved significantly in 1997, but deteriorated slightly during 1998 and 1999 (Figure 3.6).[20] The combined cash-flow results of Berne Union members have been in surplus since 1996, following negative balances since 1981.[21] The sur-

Figure 3.1. Berne Union: Structure of Export Credits, 1994–99
(Billions of U.S. dollars)

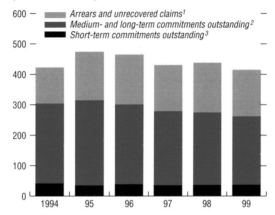

Sources: Berne Union and IMF staff estimates.

[1]Arrears and unrecovered claims: overdue payments by borrowers, classified as arrears if overdue payments have not yet resulted in claims on export credit agencies.

[2]Commitments: Total amount of loans by, or guaranteed or insured by, an export credit agency, either globally or to entities in a specific country, excluding amounts that are in arrears or on which claims have been paid. Usually includes principal and contractual interest payable by the importing country on disbursed and undisbursed credits, and sometimes includes not only liabilities of the agency but also uninsured parts of the loan.

[3]Short-term commitments: Commitments that provide repayment within a short period, usually six months. Some agencies define short-term credits as those with repayment terms of up to one or two years.

[20]Accounting practices of agencies differ, and only net cash-flow data—not accrual data—are available on a consistent basis from all export credit agencies. Assessing the financial position of export credit agencies on an accrual basis requires, among other steps, estimating the expected recovery of claims and provisioning for possible eventual losses. An increasing number of agencies have moved toward more sophisticated accounting systems, but interagency comparisons remain extremely difficult, given agencies' different accounting practices.

[21]Reflecting different accounting treatments of arrears and restructured debts, agencies that restructure an insured claim by refinancing will not reflect this refinancing in new commitments or affect the cash flow of the agency. On the other hand, for agencies that reschedule an insured claim involving a cash payment by the agency to the claimant, the cash flow would be diminished. For this reason, among others, the Berne Union data on cash-flow balances reported by the agencies should be interpreted with caution.

plus peaked at $6.1 billion in 1997; then decreased to $3.6 billion in 1999 mainly due to lower loan recovery and increased claim payments. Claims increased in 1999, reflecting payments made to exporters on cover for Indonesia and other crisis-hit countries. These business results indicate that ECAs are facing a challenge in balancing two conflicting mandates: ensuring profitability and serving as "insurers of last resort" (Box 3.1).

New Commitments and Cover Policy for Selected Countries

The export cover policy of export credit agencies significantly affects new commitments to each country—it can vary from a closed/very cautious to a very active/open stance. Business demand for insurance cover has an impact on cover policies, as plentiful business opportunities in a country stimulate export credit agencies' commercial interests to adopt an active cover policy. The macroeconomic situation of the country to be covered, the economic policy of its government, and its payments record will also affect cover policies.

The Asian market showed mixed results during 1997–1999. For **China**, the largest recipient of new commitments, all agencies remained open for business, generally without restrictions. However new commitments, which reached $17 billion in 1997, fell to $8½ billion in 1999. Agencies' payments experience was generally positive, thus agencies were open for short- and medium-/long-term business with bank or sovereign guarantees. New commitments to **Hong Kong SAR** also have continued to slow since 1997. New commitments to **India** and **Malaysia** marked significant increases: new commitments to India increased by 2 percent in 1998 and 19 percent in 1999, reflecting new business related to large-scale private power sector projects. After India conducted nuclear tests in 1998, some agencies had tightened their cover policies temporarily. With Malaysia's economic recovery, new commitments increased by 43 percent in 1999, after decreasing

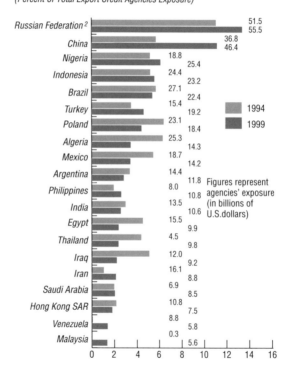

Figure 3.2. Exposure of Export Credit Agencies to Selected Major Developing Countries[1] and Countries in Transition, 1994 and 1999
(Percent of Total Export Credit Agencies Exposure)

Sources: Berne Union and IMF staff estimates.
[1]Berne Union reporting agencies.
[2]Includes debts of the former USSR.

Figure 3.3 Officially Supported Export Credits: New Commitments, 1995–99
(Billions of U.S. dollars)

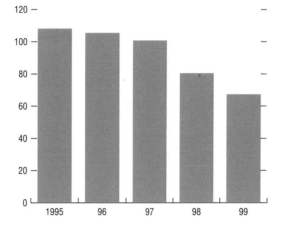

Source: Berne Union.

Figure 3.4. New Export Credit Commitments in Selected Major Markets, 1995–99
(Billions of U.S. dollars)

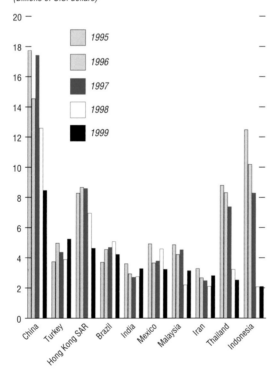

Sources: Berne Union and IMF staff estimates.

by 52 percent in 1998. Demand for export credit cover still remains fragile for other Asian countries: in **Indonesia**, which was the second largest recipient of new cover in 1997, new commitments decreased by 75 percent from 1997 to 1999. Many agencies reported arrears and restructuring operations in Indonesia; hence, cover policies remained restrictive. New commitments to **Thailand** and **Philippines** declined by 22 percent and 16 percent, respectively, in 1999.

The ECAs remained open for business, generally without restrictions, to three major Latin American markets (Brazil, Mexico, Argentina); however, new commitments to those three markets declined significantly in 1999 after some increase in 1998. This reflected mainly projects concentrated in the preceding year. Agencies eased restrictions on business with the public sector in Brazil.

For other markets, the ECAs generally eased cover policy to Turkey, Iran, and Egypt, while they maintained tight policies on Pakistan and Russia. New cover for Turkey fell by 11 percent in 1998, but increased by 35 percent in 1999, reflecting buoyant demand for new business related to large-scale power and infrastructure projects. Agencies experienced a good payments behavior as well as a significant increase in applications for new business. A decline in new commitments to **Iran** and **Egypt** in 1998 by 15 percent and 4 percent, respectively, was followed by increases of 34 percent and 23 percent in 1999, reflecting strong demand for cover and an easing in cover policies. New commitments to **Saudi Arabia** increased by 119 percent in 1998, before falling by 49 percent in 1999. Agencies were generally cautious on **Russia**; some agencies remained off cover for medium- and long-term transactions, while others were open only with a sovereign guarantee and with limits on new business. This caution has been reinforced by the Russian crisis and debt-servicing difficulties that started in mid-1998. The agencies generally maintained tight cover policy on **Pakistan** due to the deteriorating macroeconomic situation and economic policies perceived as not conducive to foreign investments.[22]

Institutional Changes

In April 1999, a system to determine minimum country risk premium rates for medium- and long-term export credit cover, known as the "Knaepen Package," came into effect. The Knaepen Package was agreed in 1997 and has been incorporated into the *Arrangement on Guidelines for Officially Supported Export Credits* (OECD Consensus). It lays down the basic rules on export credit pricing that help to eliminate subsidies and trade distortions by defining minimum premium rates for country and sovereign risk (Box 3.2). All ECAs in the participant countries of the OECD Consensus have adjusted their risk premium structures accordingly.

Also in 1999, the Working Party on Export Credits and Credit Guarantees (ECG) of the OECD concluded the Agreement on Environmental Information, which provides a basis for the export credit agencies involved in financing environmentally sensitive projects to share information, including environmental impact assessments, and to coordinate their responses to exporters and other parties. This agreement institutionalized the exchange of such information under the previous agreement in 1997, which were on a case-by-case and voluntary basis. Within the framework of the OECD, work continues to formulate common environmental guidelines for ECAs, and most ECAs have adopted or are considering internal environmental standards.

---

[22]The Pakistani government and Power Development Authority questioned the legitimacy of power purchase agreements concluded with private generating companies whose power plants had been financed with project loans from abroad. The government sought renegotiation of the tariff level in the agreements on governance grounds. By end-1999, six private power companies had agreed to a tariff reduction, and by end-2000 all power sector disputes were settled.

Figure 3.5. Main Recipients of Export Credits Among Developing Countries and Countries in Transition, 1999[1]
(Percent share of export credits in total external debt)

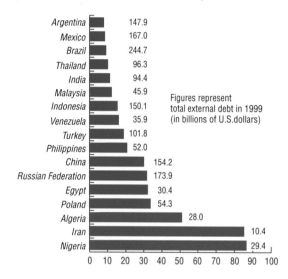

Figures represent total external debt in 1999 (in billions of U.S.dollars)

Argentina	147.9
Mexico	167.0
Brazil	244.7
Thailand	96.3
India	94.4
Malaysia	45.9
Indonesia	150.1
Venezuela	35.9
Turkey	101.8
Philippines	52.0
China	154.2
Russian Federation	173.9
Egypt	30.4
Poland	54.3
Algeria	28.0
Iran	10.4
Nigeria	29.4

Sources: Berne Union and IMF staff estimates.
[1]Data for stocks of debt of Hong Kong SAR, Saudi Arabia, and Iraq are not available.

Figure 3.6. Export Credit Agencies: Premium Income, Recoveries, Claims, and Net Cash Flow, 1994–99
(Billions of U.S. dollars)

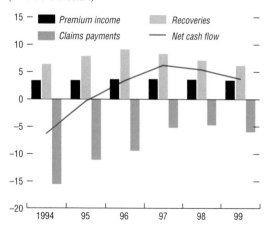

- Premium income
- Claims payments
- Recoveries
- Net cash flow

Source: Berne Union.

Box 3.1. The Changing Role of Export Credit Agencies[1]

The primary motivation of governments to set up export credit agencies (ECAs) is the stimulation of exports. While long the domain of official ECAs, since the early 1990s the private sector has been willing to underwrite political risks on a substantial and growing scale. This has left many ECAs wrestling with the practicalities of operating under two seemingly conflicting objectives: on the one hand, ECAs need to break even; on the other, these agencies remain "insurers of last resort." As a result, official ECAs have been subject to changes that in recent years have been more rapid, more frequent, and more significant than before.

- The new techniques developed for increasing private sector insurance against risk of natural catastrophes such as hurricanes and tidal waves (through bond issuance or alternative risk transfer mechanisms) are being applied to the area of political risk insurance: private insurers and reinsurers in the 1990s have entered into the political risk cover business without seeking any involvement from official export credit agencies.

- It is estimated that about 20 private underwriters are offering credit insurance cover in the London market alone, and between 85 and 95 percent of short-term export credit insurance business within and beyond the European Union is now underwritten by private insurers, without the involvement of governments.

- An increasingly large percentage of project business is structured on a private sector or privatized basis, partly because of disenchantment with sovereign guarantees in recipient countries. Project financing presents a wide range of challenges and problems for ECAs and other parties concerned. In such projects, many different agencies of the host governments can play varying roles: the viability of a project can depend

on certain tax breaks; the project may depend on an export license; the government may be the supplier of crucial fuel or the main purchaser of a project's output. Thus it has been increasingly difficult for ECAs to minimize the documentation risks by specifying the risks covered in their undertakings.

- In the arrangements for project financing, ECAs and banks have conflicting objectives: banks would prefer a risk-sharing approach that specifies the risks not covered by the ECA facility, while ECAs prefer listing only the political risks covered, with all other risks considered to be commercial and thus assumed by banks. In addition, documentation risks used to be borne by exporters and their banks; however, ECAs recently have needed to address this issue at the early stages of a contract, reflecting the complexity of risk-sharing schemes in the related financing arrangements.

- In the past, debt problems have mostly related to medium- and long-term public sector or sovereign debt, and the Paris Club and London Club have been forums for debt negotiation. However, in the future, debt problems may arise in countries where most of the debt is short-term private sector debt or related to large project financing. In such cases, different debt-workout mechanisms may be required.

- Considerable work has been done to develop minimum premium rates for medium- and long-term political risks within the OECD. However, the minimum premium rates adopted reflect a compromise, and hence, over the next few years, ECAs need to develop systems to ensure an actuarial relationship between risks and the rates they charge. This has become more difficult as forecasting default has become increasingly complex with the possibility of sudden and substantial foreign exchange outflows, reflecting short-term capital movements in a liberalized world.

[1]See Stephens (1999).

Box 3.2. Main Elements of the Knaepen Package

Minimum premium: The Guiding Principles set a benchmark system of minimum premium rates that correspond to country risk categories. The benchmark premium rate applies to both sovereign and country credit risk, irrespective of whether the buyer or borrower is a public or private entity. The benchmarks vary depending on the disbursement periods, repayment periods, and currencies. The benchmarks can be formulated both as up-front fees and as a surcharge on the interest rates.

The Guiding Principles incorporate several mechanisms for adjusting the premium level, reflecting the differences in the percentage of coverage. If only country risk is covered, 90 percent of the benchmark rate is applied. Another premium adjusting element to be considered is the coverage of the interest during the claim waiting period. If the ECA's coverage of the interest during this period requires a premium surcharge, a discount is applied to the benchmark to avoid excessive surcharges. Each ECA is to adjust its respective premium table to reflect these principles. It has been agreed that the benchmark rates will be subject to review and adjustment with reference to (1) financial results of the ECAs (details to be determined), and (2) appropriate private market indicators for country risk premia such as bond market spreads or syndicated loan market spreads.

Country risk categories: A working group of experts from various ECAs has been formed to maintain the rating system for country risk. The Belgian ECA (Office National du Ducroire—OND) serves as a secretariat for this task and maintains a model for country risk assessment. The model uses the risk-scoring methods based on quantitative indicators covering payment experience, financial and economic data, and the political situation. It was agreed that the OND update the model quarterly and electronically transmit the results to the group of risk assessment experts. The results will provide a platform for discussions to be held three times a year. These qualitative reviews determine any major changes in country risk assessments.

Transparency: The formula to determine minimum premium benchmarks for the individual risk categories has been incorporated into the text of the OECD guidelines and published. Several ECAs provide premium calculators on their websites. However, some minor differences among the minimum benchmarks applied by the individual ECAs still exist, reflecting differences in the provision of export credit facilities. ECAs will have to adjust their individual premium systems to conform to the standard set by the Guiding Principles. It was also agreed that the electronic exchange of information would facilitate information flows.

The table on the next page shows the JBIC premium rate system (Japan Bank for international Cooperation website (*http://www.jbic.go.jp*) as an example that has conformed to the standard.

The OECD Council has identified the Agriculture Sector Arrangement as a priority agenda for the ECG. The current Consensus explicitly excludes agricultural products and military sales from its scope. However, the Uruguay Round has mandated the formulation of a sector understanding covering agriculture. In the communiqué of the May 1999 OECD Ministerial Meeting, ministers expressed regret that the participants in the Consensus had not yet reached an agreement on the agriculture sector understanding and urged efforts to conclude it promptly.

Regarding changes in individual ECAs, during 1999–2000, the Japanese government undertook a comprehensive reform of the official export credit program in the broader context of administrative and fiscal reform. In

Box 3.2 *(concluded)*

JBIC Country Risk Category Upfront Rates and Country Risk Classification as of November 2000
(Percent)

Repayment period	1	2	3	4	5	6	7
5 years	1.05	1.91	3.12	4.60	6.40	8.22	10.38
8.5 years	1.42	2.75	4.57	6.79	9.38	11.93	14.86
10 years	1.58	3.10	5.19	7.73	10.66	13.51	16.78
12 years	1.79	3.58	6.02	8.98	12.36	15.63	19.34
15 years	2.11	4.29	7.26	10.86	14.92	18.81	23.18

Note: Assumes a disbursement period of three years.

Country Risk Categories:

Category 1:   Brunei Darussalam, Singapore, Taiwan Province of China.

Category 2:   Botswana, Chile, China, Czech Republic, Hong Kong SAR, Hungary, Macao, Malaysia, Poland, Slovenia, Trinidad and Tobago, UAE.

Category 3:   Bahamas, Bahrain, Costa Rica, Cyprus, Estonia, India, Israel, Kuwait, Malta, Mauritius, Mexico, Philippines, Saudi Arabia, Slovakia, Thailand, Tunisia, Uruguay.

Category 4:   Aruba, Croatia, Egypt, El Salvador, Latvia, Morocco, Oman, Panama, Quatar, St. Kitts and Nevis, South Africa.

Category 5:   Algeria, Bangladesh, Belize, Colombia, Dominica, Iran, Jamaica, Lithuania, Maldives, Papua New Guinea, Peru, Sri Lanka, Turkey, Venezuela.

Category 6:   Argentina, Benin, Bhutan, Bolivia, Brazil, Bulgaria, Cape Verde, Gabon, Ghana, Guatemala, Jordan, Kazakhstan, Kenya, Lesotho, Nepal, Netherlands Antilles, Paraguay, Romania, Russia, Senegal, Vietnam

Category 7:   Albania, Angola, Antigua and Barbuda, Armenia, Azerbaijan, Belarus, Bolivia, Bosnia and Herzegovina, Burkina Faso, Cameroon, Central African Republic, Chad, Côte d'Ivoire, Cuba, Democratic Republic of Congo, Ecuador, Ethiopia, Equatorial Guinea, Gambia, Georgia, Guinea, Guinea-Bissau, Guyana, Haiti, Honduras, Iraq, Kyrgyz Republic, Laos, Libya, Liberia, Macedonia, Madagascar, Malawi, Mali, Mauritania, Moldova, Mongolia, Myanmar, Mozambique, Nicaragua, Niger, Nigeria, North Korea, Pakistan, Rwanda, Republic of Congo, São Tomé and Príncipe, Seychelles, Sierra Leone, Somalia, St. Vincent and the Grenadines, Sudan, Suriname, Syrian Arab Republic, Tajikistan, Tanzania, Togo, Turkmenistan, Uganda, Ukraine, Uzbekistan, Yemen, Zambia, Zimbabwe.

October 1999, the Japan Bank for International Cooperation (JBIC) was established through a merger of the Export-Import Bank of Japan and the Overseas Economic Cooperation Fund. In April 2001, the export insurance division of the Ministry of Economy, Trade, and Industry was transformed into an independent agency. This is part of a comprehensive reform of the Fiscal Investment and Loan Program that came into effect in April 2001. These reforms aim at strengthening the corporate governance structure of public agencies and extending financial autonomy to those institutions (Box 3.3).

Box 3. 3 Comprehensive Reform of the Japanese Official Export Credit System

On October 1, 1999, the Japan Bank for International Cooperation (JBIC) was established through a merger of the Export-Import Bank of Japan (JEXIM) and the Overseas Economic Cooperation Fund (OECF). This merger was part of a comprehensive civil service reform in Japan approved by the Cabinet in March 1995. In April 1999, the Diet approved "The Japan Bank of International Cooperation Law," which stipulates the mission and the operational principles of the new institution. According to Article 1 of the new law, the purpose of the JBIC is to contribute to the sound development of Japan and the international economy through lending and other financial operations in order to promote exports, imports, or Japanese economic activities abroad, to facilitate stability in developing countries, and to support self-reliant development efforts in developing countries. The article also stipulates that the JBIC shall not compete with commercial financial institutions.

The functions performed by the JEXIM and the OECF have been carried over to the new JBIC. Under the previous system, t he JEXIM's main function was non-ODA official lending in the areas of export credit, import credit, foreign direct investment loans, and untied loans, while OECF extended mainly ODA loans. The JBIC's operations are classified into two broad categories: "international financial operations"—operations previously performed by JEXIM, and "overseas economic cooperation operations"—ODA operations previously performed by OECF. Reflecting the difference in the nature of the operations, separate accounts are kept. JBIC has become the largest bilateral donor agency in the world in terms of assets. As of end-March 1999, JBIC's capital was ¥6.4 trillion ($60 billion), and total assets amounted to ¥21.8 trillion ($204 billion). The total staff numbers less than 900.

As of April 2001, an independent public agency (with financial autonomy) took over charge of the export insurance activities currently operated by the export insurance division of the Ministry of Economy, Trade, and Industry.

The Japanese government has also decided to implement a fundamental reform of the Fiscal Investment and Loan Program (FILP). Currently resources in the postal savings and pension reserves must be deposited in the Trust Fund Bureau account. The JBIC (for both non-concessional lending and concessional lending) and the other FILP agencies, such as the Housing Loan Corporation and the Development Bank of Japan, rely heavily upon this fund pooling as their primary fund resource. The bill will terminate this compulsory fund pooling and all FILP agencies will issue bonds in the market. The Trust Fund Bureau account may purchase these bonds on market terms. Thus, all FILP agencies will be exposed to market discipline, and the corporate governance of the FILP agencies is expected to strengthen. This will require of FILP agencies a higher degree of accountability for their operation.

Multilateral lending to developing countries (both in gross and net terms) increased substantially in 1997 and 1998 (Table 4.1), as large financing packages were extended to several countries afflicted by the Asian financial crisis of 1997. Total gross lending by multilaterals increased from $43 billion in 1996 to $64 billion in 1997 and $76 billion in 1998, while net disbursements more than tripled during this period. Four East Asian countries—Thailand, Indonesia, Philippines, and South Korea—together accounted for 40 percent of the total lending to developing countries in 1997 and 32 percent in 1998. Lending to Brazil jumped from $2.7 billion in 1997 to $11.7 billion in 1998, when it experienced balance of payments difficulties as confidence faltered in emerging market economies following the Russian default on external debt service obligations (Table 4.2).

In 1999, as the crisis-affected countries began to recover, the need for multilateral borrowing declined significantly. Gross multilateral lending fell to $53 billion, while net lending declined even more steeply, from its peak of $47 billion in 1998 to $6 billion in 1999. The latter reflected, among other things, large prepayments to the IMF by South Korea, made possible by its rapid economic recovery.

Multilateral lending remained the dominant financing source for heavily indebted poor countries (HIPCs), which have limited market access. Multilateral assistance to HIPCs is expected to increase over the coming years, as countries benefit both from lending by multilateral agencies and from assistance under the enhanced HIPC Initiative.

The regional distribution of new multilateral lending reflects assistance provided to crisis countries (Table 4.3). Gross multilateral lending to the East Asian region increased from less than $7 billion in 1996 to nearly $30 billion in 1997 and 1998. However, as these countries began to recover, multilateral lending declined to about $11 billion in 1999. The fluctuations in net disbursements to East Asian countries were even stronger: they jumped from about $1 billion in 1996 to $26 billion in 1997 and $22 billion in 1998, before turning negative in 1999. Gross multilateral lending to the Western Hemisphere region, which had declined to about $11 billion after the Mexican crisis of 1995, rose to almost $23 billion in 1998 and 1999, reflecting mainly the impact of a support package for Brazil. At the same time, disbursements to sub-Saharan Africa, and North Africa and the Middle East have been declining since 1996.

The overall share of multilateral creditors in total lending to developing countries increased significantly in 1997 and 1998 compared with 1996. The share of the IMF in multilateral lending more than doubled (Table 4.1) during these years, reflecting the large lending to the countries affected by the financial crisis. This support lending helped to replace partially the rapid outflow of private capital, and mirrored the surge in multilateral lending in 1995 when Mexico and Russia experienced crises. Gross financial assistance provided by the IMF in the context of Fund-supported programs during 1997 and 1998 increased to about $23 billion and $29 billion, respectively, from less than $9 billion in 1996. The assistance fell back to about $15 billion in 1999. Net flows increased from $1 billion in 1996 to about $15 billion in 1997 and $19 billion in 1998, before turning negative ($13 billion) in 1999. Most of the strong increase in the disbursements in 1998–99 was related to the stand-by and extended arrangements concluded with Brazil, Indonesia, Korea, Russia, and Thailand.

Table 4.1. Developing Countries: Gross and Net Disbursements on Public External Debt[1]

	Gross Disbursements							Net Disbursements						
	Annual average		1995	1996	1997	1998	1999	Annual average		1995	1996	1997	1998	1999
	1985–89	1990–94						1985–89	1990–94					
	(Billions of U.S. dollars)													
All developing countries[1]	107.0	124.0	172.2	173.7	200.8	206.0	167.1	36.9	40.3	63.7	46.0	64.3	86.3	5.4
Multilateral	25.7	36.9	60.2	42.5	64.2	75.6	53.2	9.1	14.8	27.8	13.9	35.8	46.9	6.1
IMF	4.7	8.1	27.9	8.7	23.2	29.1	14.7	−3.2	1.5	16.8	1.0	14.7	19.2	−12.6
Other	21.0	28.9	32.3	33.8	41.0	46.5	38.6	12.3	13.3	11.0	12.8	21.2	27.7	18.7
Official bilateral	22.5	23.8	33.9	22.8	24.7	22.3	24.1	11.0	10.1	10.3	−9.4	−6.7	−1.2	−1.2
Private	58.8	63.2	78.0	108.4	112.0	108.2	89.7	16.8	15.4	25.6	41.6	35.2	40.6	0.5
Middle-income countries[2]	79.9	94.9	141.3	143.6	167.2	165.3	138.7	22.3	27.2	57.8	41.4	54.2	66.0	−1.0
Multilateral	16.0	23.5	43.7	28.2	47.8	56.4	37.8	3.7	6.9	21.3	8.5	27.1	34.3	−2.0
IMF	3.5	6.0	22.9	6.4	18.6	21.6	11.0	−1.8	1.0	16.2	0.8	11.9	13.3	−14.3
Other	12.5	17.5	20.8	21.8	29.2	34.8	26.8	5.5	5.9	5.2	7.7	15.2	21.0	12.3
Official bilateral	14.5	15.7	27.2	16.1	17.4	13.7	15.8	5.7	5.9	10.4	−9.3	−6.0	−3.6	−4.6
Private	49.5	55.7	70.4	99.3	102.0	95.3	85.0	12.9	14.4	26.1	42.2	33.1	35.3	5.5
Low-income countries[3]	27.0	29.1	30.9	30.2	33.6	40.7	28.5	14.6	13.0	6.0	4.6	10.1	20.3	6.4
Multilateral	9.7	13.4	16.5	14.3	16.3	19.2	15.5	5.4	7.9	6.4	5.4	8.7	12.6	8.1
IMF	1.2	2.1	5.0	2.2	4.6	7.6	3.7	−1.4	0.5	0.7	0.2	2.8	6.0	1.6
Other	8.5	11.4	11.5	12.0	11.8	11.6	11.8	6.7	7.4	5.8	5.1	6.0	6.7	6.4
Official bilateral	8.1	8.1	6.7	6.7	7.3	8.5	8.3	5.3	4.2	0.0	−0.1	−0.7	2.4	3.3
Private	9.3	7.6	7.6	9.2	10.0	12.9	4.7	3.9	1.0	−0.5	−0.7	2.1	5.3	−5.0
Heavily indebted poor countries[4]	10.2	8.8	10.6	8.5	9.4	7.8	7.4	6.3	5.1	3.9	3.3	4.1	2.6	1.7
Multilateral	4.2	5.2	7.5	5.8	6.0	5.1	4.9	2.3	3.1	3.3	3.3	3.6	2.7	2.8
IMF	0.8	0.7	3.0	1.0	0.7	1.0	0.8	−0.3	0.0	0.6	0.3	0.0	0.2	0.2
Other	3.4	4.6	4.5	4.8	5.3	4.1	4.1	2.6	3.1	2.7	3.0	3.6	2.5	2.6
Official bilateral	3.8	2.3	1.7	1.3	1.0	1.6	1.2	3.0	1.5	0.5	0.0	0.0	0.6	0.0
Private	2.2	1.3	1.3	1.3	2.3	1.1	1.3	1.1	0.4	0.1	0.0	0.5	−0.7	−1.1
Memorandum items						(Percent of total)								
All developing countries[1]														
Multilateral	24.0	29.8	35.0	24.5	32.0	36.7	31.9	24.7	37.3	43.6	30.1	55.7	54.4	112.3
IMF	4.4	6.5	16.2	5.0	11.6	14.1	8.8	−9.1	3.7	26.4	2.2	22.8	22.3	−232.6
Other	19.6	23.3	18.8	19.5	20.4	22.5	23.1	33.8	33.5	17.2	27.9	32.9	32.1	344.9
Official bilateral	21.1	19.3	19.7	13.1	12.3	10.8	14.4	30.5	25.4	16.2	−20.4	−10.4	−1.4	−22.3
Private	55.0	50.9	45.3	62.4	55.8	52.5	53.7	44.8	37.3	40.2	90.3	54.7	47.1	10.0
						(Billions of U.S. dollars)								
Private nonguaranteed debt[5]														
All developing countries[1]	9.2	36.9	68.5	100.7	124.0	123.1	104.0	−1.7	18.9	37.4	57.1	61.7	47.3	−1.2
Middle-income countries[2]	7.0	31.3	59.2	84.9	107.8	117.7	100.1	−2.2	16.7	33.4	49.1	54.0	50.8	4.1
Low-income countries[3]	2.2	5.7	9.3	15.9	16.2	5.4	3.9	0.5	2.2	4.0	8.0	7.7	−3.5	−5.4
Heavily indebted poor countries[4]	0.5	0.4	0.2	0.9	0.5	0.4	n.a.	0.0	0.0	0.0	0.4	−0.1	−0.1	−0.2

Sources: World Bank Debtor Reporting System (DRS) and *Global Development Finance* (GDF); and IMF, *International Financial Statistics* (various issues).

Note: Disbursements on medium- and long-term public and publicly guaranteed debt, including to the IMF. Differences in coverage and definitions make the World Bank data presented in this table incompatible with OECD data. GDF aggregate estimates are used except for HIPC aggregates. IMF data are used for IMF indicators for 1999.

[1]A group of 149 countries covered by the GDF. Of these, 137 report to the DRS, while World Bank estimates are used for the others.

[2]A group of 85 countries covered by the GDF for which 1999 GNP per capita was between $756 and $9,265 as calculated by the World Bank. Seventy-five countries report to the DRS, and World Bank estimates are used for the others.

[3]A group of 64 countries for which 1999 GNP per capita was no more than $755 as calculated by the World Bank. Of these, 62 report to the DRS.

[4]A group of 41 countries.

[5]Not all countries report their private nonguaranteed debt to the DRS; World Bank estimates are used where this type of debt is not reported but known to be significant.

Table 4.2. Selected Countries: Gross and Net Disbursements on Public External Debt[1]
(Billions of U.S. dollars)

	Gross Disbursements					Net Disbursements				
	1995	1996	1997	1998	1999	1995	1996	1997	1998	1999
Middle-income countries[2]	141.3	143.6	167.2	165.3	138.7	57.8	41.4	54.2	66.0	−1.0
Multilateral	43.7	28.2	47.8	56.4	37.8	21.3	8.5	27.1	34.3	−2.0
IMF	22.9	6.4	18.6	21.6	11.0	16.2	0.8	11.9	13.3	−14.3
Other	20.8	21.8	29.2	34.8	26.8	5.2	7.7	15.2	21.0	12.3
Official bilateral	27.2	16.1	17.4	13.7	15.8	10.4	−9.3	−6.0	−3.6	−4.6
Private	70.4	99.3	102.0	95.3	85.0	26.1	42.2	33.1	35.3	5.5
Thailand	2.8	2.6	10.6	5.6	3.8	0.9	1.3	9.4	4.6	1.2
Multilateral	0.4	0.3	3.5	1.8	1.4	0.0	0.0	3.3	1.6	1.1
IMF	0.0	0.0	2.5	0.7	0.3	0.0	0.0	2.5	0.7	0.3
Other	0.4	0.3	1.1	1.1	1.1	0.0	0.0	0.8	0.9	0.8
Official bilateral	1.1	1.1	5.5	0.7	2.0	0.5	0.4	5.1	0.2	1.4
Private	1.3	1.2	1.5	3.1	0.4	0.4	0.9	1.0	2.8	−1.2
Indonesia	6.7	7.5	9.3	13.2	7.2	1.0	−0.6	3.6	9.0	1.7
Multilateral	1.8	1.7	4.6	8.1	3.9	0.5	−1.3	3.0	7.2	2.9
IMF	0.0	0.0	3.0	5.8	1.4	0.0	0.0	3.0	5.8	1.4
Other	1.8	1.7	1.6	2.4	2.6	0.5	−1.3	−0.1	1.4	1.5
Official bilateral	2.5	2.3	2.4	2.9	2.9	0.6	0.5	0.6	1.3	1.6
Private	2.4	3.6	2.3	2.2	0.4	−0.2	0.2	0.1	0.5	−2.7
Mexico	36.7	22.9	15.3	13.2	10.8	26.4	0.6	−10.1	0.5	−4.1
Multilateral	16.0	2.1	1.5	1.9	2.7	13.1	−1.7	−3.6	−0.8	−4.0
IMF	13.3	0.0	0.0	0.0	1.4	12.1	−2.1	−3.4	−1.1	−3.7
Other	2.7	2.1	1.5	1.9	1.3	1.0	0.4	−0.1	0.3	−0.4
Official bilateral	10.8	0.4	0.2	0.3	0.1	9.4	−8.0	−4.5	−1.1	−1.3
Private	10.0	20.5	13.6	11.0	7.9	3.9	10.2	−2.1	2.4	1.3
Philippines	1.8	3.2	3.9	3.4	7.6	−1.1	0.3	1.8	0.8	4.1
Multilateral	0.6	0.7	1.3	1.4	0.6	−0.4	−0.2	0.5	0.7	0.0
IMF	0.0	0.0	0.7	0.7	0.3	−0.4	−0.3	0.5	0.7	0.3
Other	0.6	0.7	0.6	0.7	0.3	0.0	0.1	0.0	0.1	−0.3
Official bilateral	0.8	0.9	1.2	0.8	1.3	−0.7	−0.1	0.1	−0.1	0.2
Private	0.4	1.6	1.4	1.3	5.7	0.0	0.7	1.2	0.1	3.9
Russian Federation	8.5	10.1	8.9	20.7	2.6	5.3	7.0	7.1	16.0	−3.5
Multilateral	6.3	4.9	4.8	7.5	1.2	5.9	4.1	4.2	6.5	−3.2
IMF	5.5	3.8	2.0	6.2	0.6	5.5	3.2	1.5	5.3	−3.6
Other	0.9	1.2	2.7	1.3	0.6	0.4	0.9	2.7	1.2	0.4
Official bilateral	0.1	2.9	0.3	0.6	0.7	−0.4	2.7	−0.1	−0.5	0.2
Private	2.1	2.3	3.9	12.5	0.7	−0.3	0.2	3.0	10.0	−0.5
South Korea	5.2	7.1	26.1	20.5	11.6	2.2	3.3	23.3	14.9	−17.9
Multilateral	0.2	0.2	16.4	12.8	1.6	−0.4	−0.3	16.0	9.7	−9.5
IMF	0.0	0.0	11.3	7.9	0.5	0.0	0.0	11.3	5.2	−10.3
Other	0.2	0.2	5.2	4.8	1.1	−0.4	−0.3	4.7	4.5	0.8
Official bilateral	0.0	0.0	0.0	1.0	3.5	−0.3	−0.2	−0.2	1.0	2.5
Private	5.0	6.9	9.6	6.7	6.6	2.8	3.8	7.5	4.2	−10.9
Brazil	7.9	10.2	10.5	24.2	19.7	1.5	3.3	−0.1	14.3	0.1
Multilateral	1.3	2.3	2.7	11.7	10.7	−0.5	0.7	1.4	10.4	6.1
IMF	0.0	0.0	0.0	4.6	6.1	0.0	−0.1	0.0	4.6	4.1
Other	1.3	2.3	2.7	7.0	4.6	−0.4	0.7	1.4	5.8	2.0
Official bilateral	0.7	0.9	0.3	2.4	0.7	−1.1	−1.0	−2.6	0.2	−1.3
Private	5.9	7.0	7.5	10.1	8.3	3.1	3.6	1.1	3.8	−4.6

Sources: World Bank Debtor Reporting System (DRS) and Global Development Finance (GDF); and IMF, *International Financial Statistics* (various issues).

[1]Disbursements on medium- and long-term public and publicly guaranteed debt, including to the IMF. Differences in coverage and definitions make the World Bank data presented in this table incompatible with OECD data. GDF aggregate estimates are used except for HIPC aggregates. IMF data are used for IMF indicators for 1999.

[2]A group of 85 countries covered by the GDF for which 1999 GNP per capita was between $756 and $9,265 as calculated by the World Bank. Seventy-five countries report to the DRS, and World Bank estimates are used for the others.

Table 4.3. Developing Countries: Gross and Net Disbursements from Multilateral Institutions by Region

	Gross Disbursements							Net Disbursements						
	Annual average							Annual average						
	1985–89	1990–94	1995	1996	1997	1998	1999	1985–89	1990–94	1995	1996	1997	1998	1999
	(Billions of U.S. dollars)													
All developing countries[1]	25.7	36.9	60.2	42.5	64.2	75.6	53.2	9.1	14.8	27.8	13.9	35.8	46.9	6.1
IMF	4.7	8.1	27.9	8.7	23.2	29.1	14.7	–3.2	1.5	16.8	1.0	14.7	19.2	–12.6
Other	21.0	28.9	32.3	33.8	41.0	46.5	38.6	12.3	13.3	11.0	12.8	21.2	27.7	18.7
Sub-Saharan Africa	4.3	5.5	7.2	4.8	4.6	4.2	3.6	2.3	3.3	2.8	2.2	1.6	1.3	1.1
IMF	0.8	0.8	3.0	0.6	0.5	0.8	0.5	–0.3	0.2	0.6	0.1	–0.5	–0.3	–0.1
Other	3.5	4.7	4.2	4.2	4.1	3.4	3.1	2.7	3.1	2.2	2.2	2.1	1.6	1.2
North Africa and the Middle East	2.2	3.1	4.0	4.5	3.6	3.0	3.3	1.0	1.1	1.5	2.3	0.5	0.4	0.6
IMF	0.4	0.4	0.6	1.0	0.7	0.5	0.5	0.0	0.0	0.2	0.7	0.3	0.0	0.0
Other	1.8	2.7	3.4	3.5	2.9	2.5	2.8	1.0	1.1	1.3	1.6	0.2	0.5	0.6
East Asia and the Pacific	4.6	5.8	6.5	6.6	29.7	28.0	10.6	1.4	2.0	2.5	1.2	25.7	22.1	–3.5
IMF	0.6	0.3	0.2	0.2	17.5	15.1	2.5	–0.6	–0.4	–0.2	–0.1	17.2	12.2	–8.4
Other	4.0	5.5	6.3	6.4	12.2	12.9	8.1	2.0	2.3	2.7	1.3	8.4	10.0	4.9
South Asia	3.8	6.0	4.2	4.8	4.4	4.4	5.0	1.8	3.8	0.0	1.5	1.2	1.7	1.8
IMF	0.3	1.3	0.2	0.2	0.3	0.3	0.6	–1.0	0.5	–1.8	–1.3	–0.8	–0.4	–0.2
Other	3.4	4.7	4.0	4.6	4.1	4.1	4.3	2.9	3.3	1.7	2.7	2.1	2.1	2.0
Western Hemisphere	8.5	10.5	25.8	11.1	12.0	22.6	22.5	3.1	1.1	14.6	0.6	0.4	13.9	6.1
IMF	2.3	2.6	15.8	1.5	0.8	5.0	7.7	–0.1	–0.7	12.9	–2.0	–3.9	2.5	–0.9
Other	6.2	7.9	10.0	9.6	11.2	17.5	14.8	3.2	1.8	1.7	2.6	4.3	11.3	7.0
Europe and Central Asia	2.2	6.0	12.6	10.7	9.9	13.4	8.3	–0.5	3.6	6.5	6.1	6.5	7.6	0.0
IMF	0.2	2.7	8.2	5.2	3.4	7.4	2.8	–1.1	2.0	5.1	3.7	2.4	5.3	–3.1
Other	2.0	3.3	4.4	5.5	6.5	6.0	5.4	0.6	1.6	1.4	2.4	4.1	2.2	3.1
	(Percent of total)													
Sub-Saharan Africa	17	15	12	11	7	6	7	28	23	10	16	4	3	18
North Africa and the Middle East	9	8	7	11	6	4	6	12	8	5	16	1	1	10
East Asia and the Pacific	18	16	11	16	46	37	20	14	13	9	9	72	47	–57
South Asia	14	16	7	11	7	6	9	22	26	0	11	3	4	29
Western Hemisphere	33	28	43	26	19	30	42	33	6	52	4	1	30	99
Europe and Central Asia	9	16	21	25	15	18	15	–9	25	23	44	18	16	0

Sources: World Bank Debtor Reporting System (DRS) and *Global Development Finance* (GDF); and IMF, *International Financial Statistics*.
Note: Disbursements on medium- and long-term public and publicly guaranteed debt, including to the IMF. GDF aggregates are used except for IMF data for 1999.
[1]A group of 149 countries covered by the GDF. Of these, 137 report to the DRS, while World Bank estimates are used for the others.

Concessional Lending

While the Asian crisis affected nonconcessional lending, gross concessional lending from multilaterals remained flat at about $10 billion during 1997–99 (Table 4.4). The bulk of the concessional lending was directed to HIPCs and other low-income countries, similar to the trend in previous years. Net concessional lending has also remained flat in the last few years. Among the creditors, most of the concessional lending was provided by the International Development Association (IDA). The share of concessional flows to the transition economies of Europe and Central Asia declined, while flows to South Asia (for example, emergency assistance in the aftermath of natural disasters in 1998 in Bangladesh) increased. The share of sub-Saharan Africa in concessional flows increased

Table 4.4. Developing Countries: Gross and Net Disbursements from Multilateral Institutions by Concessionality

	Gross Disbursements							Net Disbursements						
	Annual average							Annual average						
	1985–89	1990–94	1995	1996	1997	1998	1999	1985–89	1990–94	1995	1996	1997	1998	1999
	(Billions of U.S. dollars)													
All developing countries[1]	25.7	36.9	60.2	42.5	64.2	75.6	53.2	9.1	14.8	27.8	13.9	35.8	46.9	6.1
IMF	4.7	8.1	27.9	8.7	23.2	29.1	14.7	–3.2	1.5	16.8	1.0	14.7	19.2	–12.6
Other	21.0	28.9	32.3	33.8	41.0	46.5	38.6	12.3	13.3	11.0	12.8	21.2	27.7	18.7
Concessional	6.0	8.7	11.0	11.0	10.2	10.1	9.8	4.8	7.3	8.8	8.6	7.6	7.3	6.9
IMF[2]	0.5	0.8	2.2	1.0	1.0	1.2	1.0	–0.1	0.6	1.6	0.3	0.2	0.4	0.2
Other	5.5	7.8	8.8	10.0	9.2	8.9	8.8	4.9	6.6	7.2	8.2	7.4	6.9	6.7
Nonconcessional	19.7	28.2	49.2	31.5	54.0	65.5	43.4	4.3	7.5	18.9	5.3	28.3	39.6	–0.8
Middle-income countries[3]	16.0	23.5	43.7	28.2	47.8	56.4	37.8	3.7	6.9	21.3	8.5	27.1	34.3	–2.0
IMF	3.5	6.0	22.9	6.4	18.6	21.6	11.0	–1.8	1.0	16.2	0.8	11.9	13.3	–14.3
Other	12.5	17.5	20.8	21.8	29.2	34.8	26.8	5.5	5.9	5.2	7.7	15.2	21.0	12.3
Concessional	1.4	2.3	2.6	3.0	2.6	2.4	2.7	0.9	1.8	2.0	2.2	1.8	1.5	1.8
IMF[2]	0.1	0.2	0.1	0.1	0.1	0.1	0.2	–0.2	0.1	0.0	0.0	0.0	–0.1	0.0
Other	1.3	2.1	2.6	2.9	2.5	2.3	2.5	1.1	1.6	2.0	2.2	1.8	1.6	1.8
Nonconcessional	14.6	21.2	41.0	25.2	45.3	53.9	35.1	2.8	5.1	19.3	6.3	25.3	32.8	–3.7
Low-income countries[4]	9.7	13.4	16.5	14.3	16.3	19.2	15.5	5.4	7.9	6.4	5.4	8.7	12.6	8.1
IMF	1.2	2.1	5.0	2.2	4.6	7.6	3.7	–1.4	0.5	0.7	0.2	2.8	6.0	1.6
Other	8.5	11.4	11.5	12.0	11.8	11.6	11.8	6.7	7.4	5.8	5.1	6.0	6.7	6.4
Concessional	4.6	6.4	8.3	8.0	7.6	7.7	7.1	3.9	5.5	6.8	6.3	5.8	5.8	5.1
IMF[2]	0.4	0.7	2.1	1.0	0.9	1.1	0.8	0.1	0.5	1.6	0.3	0.2	0.4	0.2
Other	4.2	5.7	6.3	7.1	6.7	6.5	6.3	3.8	5.0	5.2	6.0	5.6	5.3	4.9
Nonconcessional	5.1	7.0	8.2	6.2	8.7	11.5	8.3	1.5	2.4	–0.3	–1.0	3.0	6.9	2.9
Heavily indebted poor countries[5]	4.2	5.2	7.5	5.8	6.0	5.1	4.9	2.3	3.1	3.3	3.3	3.6	2.7	2.8
IMF	0.8	0.7	3.0	1.0	0.7	1.0	0.8	–0.3	0.0	0.6	0.3	0.0	0.2	0.2
Other	3.4	4.6	4.5	4.8	5.3	4.1	4.1	2.6	3.1	2.7	3.0	3.6	2.5	2.6
Concessional	2.7	3.9	5.7	5.1	4.7	4.7	4.6	2.3	3.4	4.8	4.1	3.7	3.6	3.5
IMF[2]	0.3	0.5	2.0	0.8	0.6	0.9	0.8	0.1	0.4	1.6	0.4	0.1	0.3	0.3
Other	2.4	3.4	3.7	4.3	4.1	3.9	3.8	2.2	3.0	3.2	3.7	3.6	3.2	3.2
Nonconcessional	1.5	1.3	1.8	0.7	1.3	0.4	0.3	0.0	–0.3	–1.5	–0.8	–0.1	–0.9	–0.7
Concessional share in disbursements	(Percent)													
All developing countries[1]	23.2	23.5	18.3	26.0	15.9	13.4	18.4	57.8	50.8	31.8	61.8	21.1	15.6	112.8
Middle-income countries[3]	8.5	9.7	6.1	10.7	5.4	4.3	7.0	166.3	27.3	9.6	26.2	6.6	4.5	–89.0
Low-income countries[4]	48.3	47.5	50.5	56.3	46.6	40.0	46.2	73.2	71.0	105.4	118.5	66.2	45.7	63.5
Heavily indebted poor countries[5]	63.3	75.0	76.4	88.1	78.6	92.4	94.1	102.0	110.3	144.3	122.9	102.8	133.5	126.6

Sources: World Bank Debtor Reporting System (DRS) and *Global Development Finance* (GDF); and IMF, *International Financial Statistics*.
Note: Disbursements on medium- and long-term public and publicly guaranteed debt, including to the IMF. GDF data are used except for IMF, where the IMF data are used for 1999, concessional IMF lending, and HIPC data.
[1]A group of 149 countries covered by the GDF. Of these, 137 report to the DRS, while World Bank estimates are used for the others.
[2]SAF, ESAF, PRGF, and Trust Fund.
[3]A group of 85 countries covered by the GDF for which 1999 GNP per capita was between $756 and $9,265 as calculated by the World Bank. Seventy-five countries report to the DRS, and World Bank estimates are used for the others.
[4]A group of 64 countries for which 1999 GNP per capita was no more than $755 as calculated by the World Bank. Of these, 62 report to the DRS.
[5]A group of 41 countries.

somewhat in 1997 and 1998 compared with 1996. Annual IMF support on concessional terms under the Enhanced Structural Adjustment Facility (ESAF), which was replaced by the PRGF in 1999, remained at about $1 billion during 1997–99.

Multilateral Debt Service

Reflecting the new loans contracted by middle-income countries in the aftermath of the Asian financial crisis, debt service payments to

Table 4.5. Developing Countries: Multilateral Debt Service

	Annual average		1995	1996	1997	1998	1999
	1985–89	1990–94					
	(Billions of U.S. dollars)						
Multilateral debt service							
All developing countries[1]	27.4	36.9	49.2	44.7	43.4	45.7	67.0
Middle-income countries[2]	20.2	27.0	34.0	31.3	31.7	35.1	55.2
Low-income countries[3]	7.2	9.8	15.2	13.4	11.7	10.6	11.8
Heavily indebted poor countries[4]	3.0	3.5	5.7	3.7	3.6	3.4	3.1
	(Percent of exports of goods and services)						
Multilateral debt service ratio							
All developing countries[1]	4.2	3.6	3.2	2.6	2.4	2.6	3.7
Middle-income countries[2]	3.7	3.1	2.6	2.2	2.0	2.3	3.5
Low-income countries[3]	6.8	6.3	7.1	5.6	4.6	4.5	4.7
Heavily indebted poor countries[4]	11.1	9.5	11.9	6.7	6.3	5.4	4.8
	(Percent of exports of goods and services)						
Memorandum items							
Multilateral debt outstanding							
All developing countries[1]	29.3	26.6	23.0	20.5	19.7	24.8	23.7
Middle-income countries[2]	21.3	17.6	15.3	13.7	13.5	17.6	16.5
Low-income countries[3]	71.2	77.5	69.9	61.9	58.5	71.2	68.6
Heavily indebted poor countries[4]	126.7	142.5	133.4	118.4	113.3	123.9	118.9

Sources: World Bank Debtor Reporting System (DRS) and *Global Development Finance* (GDF); and IMF, *International Financial Statistics*.
Note: The numbers represent payments made. GDF aggregates are used except for 1999, where IMF data are used for debt service to the IMF. For footnotes, see Table 4.1.

multilateral institutions increased in 1999 to 3.7 percent of exports of goods and services, up from 2.4 percent in 1997 and 2.6 percent in 1998 (Table 4.5). For low-income countries and HIPCs, the debt service ratios remained well below the levels in previous years, reflecting the concessional nature of new lending. Debt service ratios of HIPCs are expected to fall further in the coming years as they benefit from debt relief under the enhanced HIPC Initiative.

Multilateral Debt

Multilateral debt of developing countries, which had grown significantly in 1995 at the time of the Mexican crisis, increased again in 1998–99. Over the last decade, total multilateral debt increased from about 21 percent of public external debt in 1990 to just over 26 percent in 1998 and 1999 (Table 4.6). For low-income countries, the share of multilateral debt grew even faster and reached more than one-third of total debt, reflecting largely their lower access to international capital markets. The IMF's share in the debt of developing countries increased from 3 percent in 1990 to almost 6 percent in 1998, reflecting the large nonconcessional crisis lending; it fell back to less than 5 percent by end-1999. For low-income countries, the share of the IMF in total debt rose from a low of 3.6 percent in 1996 to 5½ percent in 1998–99.

The World Bank remains the largest lender in absolute terms, with its share in multilateral debt at about half of the total in 1998 and 1999, up from about 39 percent in 1997 (Table 4.7). Regional development banks account for just under a quarter of developing countries' multilateral debt, and the IMF for about 20 percent.

The share of concessional debt in multilateral debt declined slightly from 34 percent in 1997 to 32 percent in 1999, reflecting the nonconcessional lending to Asian countries and Brazil in 1998–99 (Table 4.8). While for middle-income countries only about 12 percent of multilateral debt was on concessional terms in 1999, for low-income countries, it accounted for over 60 percent, and for the HIPCs 86 percent, of all debt. The IMF's concessional claims

Table 4.6. Developing Countries: Medium- and Long-Term Public External Debt by Creditor

	1980	1985	1990	1995	1996	1997	1998	1999
	(Billions of U.S. dollars)							
Public external debt								
All developing countries[1]	377	781	1,149	1,494	1,484	1,482	1,637	1,629
Middle-income countries[2]	277	601	797	1,064	1,070	1,079	1,192	1,184
Low-income countries[3]	100	180	352	430	415	403	444	445
Heavily indebted poor countries[4]	47	85	161	187	181	171	180	171
	(Percent of group total)							
All developing countries[1]								
Multilateral	16.2	18.9	21.1	23.5	23.3	24.3	26.2	26.5
IMF	3.2	5.1	3.0	4.1	4.0	4.8	5.7	4.8
Other	12.9	13.8	18.1	19.4	19.3	19.6	20.5	21.7
Official bilateral	33.6	28.4	34.5	38.4	36.7	34.1	32.3	32.7
Private	50.2	52.8	44.4	38.1	39.9	41.6	41.5	40.8
Middle-income countries[2]								
Multilateral	13.1	15.1	17.5	18.9	18.5	19.7	22.0	21.8
IMF	2.5	4.3	2.9	4.3	4.2	5.0	5.9	4.6
Other	10.6	10.8	14.5	14.6	14.3	14.7	16.1	17.3
Official bilateral	27.4	24.3	28.4	34.4	32.6	30.2	28.2	28.4
Private	59.5	60.5	54.1	46.7	48.9	50.2	49.7	49.7
Low-income countries[3]								
Multilateral	24.6	31.2	29.3	34.9	35.7	36.8	37.5	39.0
IMF	5.3	7.6	3.2	3.6	3.6	4.2	5.3	5.6
Other	19.3	23.6	26.1	31.4	32.1	32.7	32.2	33.4
Official bilateral	50.9	41.9	48.5	48.1	47.4	44.6	43.1	44.1
Private	24.5	26.9	22.2	16.9	16.9	18.5	19.3	16.9
Heavily indebted poor countries[4]								
Multilateral	25.6	29.4	28.7	34.4	36.1	38.2	38.8	41.0
IMF	7.2	7.9	4.3	4.4	4.5	4.5	4.5	4.8
Other	18.4	21.5	24.4	30.0	31.6	33.7	34.3	36.2
Official bilateral	44.2	48.8	56.1	53.4	52.6	49.8	50.0	48.5
Private	30.2	21.8	15.2	12.2	11.3	12.0	11.1	10.4

Sources: World Bank Debtor Reporting System (DRS) and *Global Development Finance* (GDF); and IMF, *International Financial Statistics*.
Note: GDF aggregate estimates are used except for 1999, where IMF data are used for the IMF. For footnotes, see Table 4.1.

on developing countries have increased slightly, from $8.2 billion in 1997 to $8.9 billion in 1998 and 1999, equivalent to about 7 percent of developing countries' concessional multilateral debt. All of this increase reflects exposure to HIPCs.

Lending Terms

Lending terms have remained broadly unchanged in recent years (Table 4.9). The World Bank offers loans with variable interest rates on nonconcessional resources, based on the cost of funding and a margin determined on the basis of a targeted net income. Borrowers from the World Bank can choose to borrow in one or

more currencies in which the Bank can fund itself, including the yen, the euro, and the U.S. dollar. Maturity on these loans is also variable, and borrowers have the flexibility to configure the grace period and maturity profile within certain limits in a manner consistent with the purpose of the loan. In some cases, they can choose to make bullet payments. Multilaterals also offer concessional resources to eligible countries through special windows, and fixed service charges are applied instead of interest rates. Concessional loans typically have a 6–10 year grace period with maturity ranging between 20 and 40 years except in the case of the IMF where concessional loans have a maturity of 10 years, with 5½ years of grace.

Table 4.7. Developing Countries: Multilateral Debt by Institution

	1980	1985	1990	1995	1996	1997	1998	1999
				(Billions of U.S. dollars)				
Total	61.0	147.3	242.3	351.3	346.4	360.6	429.4	431.9
World Bank	14.3	32.5	72.3	116.1	122.1	140.0	198.0	205.6
IBRD	2.5	8.4	27.7	45.4	47.9	63.4	114.6	118.9
IDA	11.8	24.1	44.6	70.8	74.3	76.6	83.4	86.7
Regional development banks[1]	3.0	10.2	31.9	70.9	73.5	78.8	94.6	106.2
AfDB and AfDF	0.5	1.5	7.1	15.8	16.3	15.9	17.1	17.0
AsDB	0.7	2.8	10.9	26.6	27.1	30.3	38.2	43.4
EBRD	—	—	—	0.7	1.2	1.5	2.4	2.7
IDB	1.8	5.8	13.9	27.8	28.8	31.1	36.9	43.0
European institutions	0.7	1.5	4.2	9.4	10.1	9.8	12.5	12.2
EIB and EDF	0.6	1.2	3.5	7.1	7.9	7.8	10.5	10.4
Other[2]	0.1	0.2	0.8	2.3	2.2	2.0	2.1	1.8
IMF	12.2	39.7	34.7	61.1	60.1	70.8	93.8	78.9
of which concessional	3.3	2.7	3.7	8.5	8.5	8.2	8.9	8.9
Others	30.8	63.5	99.2	93.7	80.6	61.2	30.4	29.0
				(Percent of total)				
World Bank	23.5	22.1	29.8	33.1	35.3	38.8	46.1	47.6
IBRD	4.1	5.7	11.4	12.9	13.8	17.6	26.7	27.5
IDA	19.3	16.3	18.4	20.1	21.4	21.2	19.4	20.1
Regional development banks[1]	4.9	6.9	13.2	20.2	21.2	21.8	22.0	24.6
AfDB and AfDF	0.8	1.1	2.9	4.5	4.7	4.4	4.0	3.9
AsDB	1.1	1.9	4.5	7.6	7.8	8.4	8.9	10.1
EBRD	—	—	—	0.2	0.4	0.4	0.6	0.6
IDB	2.9	4.0	5.7	7.9	8.3	8.6	8.6	10.0
European institutions	1.1	1.0	1.7	2.7	2.9	2.7	2.9	2.8
EIB and EDF	1.0	0.8	1.4	2.0	2.3	2.2	2.4	2.4
Other[2]	0.2	0.2	0.3	0.6	0.6	0.5	0.5	0.4
IMF	20.1	26.9	14.3	17.4	17.4	19.6	21.9	18.3
of which concessional[3]	27.0	6.8	10.6	13.9	14.2	11.5	9.5	11.3
Others	50.5	43.1	41.0	26.7	23.3	17.0	7.1	6.7

Sources: World Bank Debtor Reporting System (DRS) and *Global Development Finance* (GDF); IMF, *International Financial Statistics* (various issues); and IMF staff estimates.

Note: GDF aggregate data are used except for 1999, where IMF data are taken from the IMF.

Full names of institutions: AfDB—The African Development Bank, AfDF—The African Development Fund, AsDB—Asian Development Bank, EBRD—The European Bank for Reconstruction and Development, EDF—European Development Fund, EIB—European Investment Bank, IBRD—International Bank for Reconstruction and Development, IDB—The Inter-American Development Bank, IDA—International Development Association.

[1]Including development funds and other associated concessional facilities.
[2]Council of Europe and European Union.
[3]In percent of IMF total.

On average, the terms of concessional lending by multilateral institutions in 1999 comprised an interest rate of about 1.5 percent, maturity of about 25 years, and a grace period of about 7 years. The grant element calculated on these terms, using a discount rate based on commercial interest reference rates, was about 54 percent. African Development Fund (AfDF) and IDA's loans were on the most concessional terms, with a grant element of 77 percent and 72 percent, respectively. The grant element of the IMF's concessional lending was about 32 percent.

Table 4.8. Developing Countries: Multilateral Debt on Concessional Terms

	1980	1985	1990	1995	1996	1997	1998	1999
	(Billions of U.S. dollars)							
Total multilateral debt								
All developing countries[1]	61.0	147.3	242.3	351.3	346.4	360.6	429.4	431.9
Middle-income countries[2]	36.4	91.0	139.1	201.1	198.3	212.1	262.7	258.3
Low-income countries[3]	24.6	56.4	103.2	150.2	148.1	148.5	166.7	173.6
Heavily indebted poor countries[4]	12.0	25.1	46.2	64.2	65.3	65.3	70.0	70.2
Multilateral concessional debt								
All developing countries[1]	21.5	40.0	72.5	115.4	119.9	122.0	133.1	138.7
Middle-income countries[2]	6.2	10.4	15.5	25.9	27.2	27.8	30.2	31.9
Low-income countries[3]	15.4	29.5	57.0	89.6	92.6	94.3	102.9	106.8
Heavily indebted poor countries[4]	6.2	12.6	30.3	50.1	52.5	53.8	59.0	60.4
	(Percent of total multilateral debt)							
Multilateral concessional debt								
All developing countries[1]	35.3	27.1	29.9	32.9	34.6	33.8	31.0	32.1
Middle-income countries[2]	16.9	11.5	11.1	12.9	13.7	13.1	11.5	12.4
Low-income countries[3]	62.4	52.4	55.3	59.6	62.6	63.5	61.7	61.5
Heavily indebted poor countries[4]	51.4	50.3	65.5	78.0	80.5	82.5	84.3	86.0
	(Billions of U.S. dollars)							
Memorandum items								
SAF/ESAF/PRGF/Trust Fund								
All developing countries[1]	3.3	2.7	3.7	8.5	8.5	8.2	8.9	8.9
Middle-income countries[2]	1.0	1.0	0.5	1.1	1.1	1.0	0.9	0.9
Low-income countries[3]	2.3	1.7	3.2	7.4	7.5	7.2	8.0	8.0
Heavily indebted poor countries[4]	1.2	0.9	2.6	5.9	6.1	5.8	6.4	6.6
	(Percent of multilateral concessional debt)							
SAF/ESAF/PRGF/Trust Fund								
All developing countries[1]	15.4	6.7	5.0	7.3	7.1	6.7	6.7	6.4
Middle-income countries[2]	16.2	9.3	3.2	4.4	3.9	3.5	3.1	2.8
Low-income countries[3]	15.1	5.8	5.6	8.2	8.0	7.6	7.8	7.5
Heavily indebted poor countries[4]	19.7	7.0	8.5	11.8	11.6	10.8	10.9	10.9

Sources: World Bank Debtor Reporting System (DRS) and *Global Development Finance* (GDF); and IMF, *International Financial Statistics*.
Note: GDF aggregate estimates are used except for 1999 IMF data, where IMF sources are used. For footnotes, see Table 4.1.

Table 4.9. Composition and Average Terms of Multilateral Debt by Major Institutions, 1990–99

	Debt Outstanding				Average Terms of New Commitments in 1999[1]				
	Amount		Share of total					Grant element using discount rate of[2]	
	1990	1999	1990	1999	Interest	Maturity	Grace	10%	CIRRs[3]
	(Billions of U.S. dollars)		(Percent)		(Percent)	(Years)		(Percent)	
Concessional debt	72.5	138.7	100.0	100.0	1.5[4]	24.7[4]	6.8[4]	58[4]	54[4]
IDA[5]	44.6	86.7	61.5	62.5	0.8	37.7	10.0	80	72
AsDB Soft Window	6.2	16.7	8.6	12.0	2.0	33.1	8.8	66	50
AfDF	3.0	7.7	4.1	5.6	0.7	48.7	10.2	82	77
IDB Soft Window	3.9	5.8	5.3	4.2	1.9	40.0	10.5	71	66
Arab Fund for Economic and Social Development	0.9	4.0	1.3	2.9	4.5	22.6	7.9	40	33
International Fund for Agricultural Development	1.6	2.7	2.1	1.9	1.4	35.8	9.0	72	68
European Development Fund	1.5	1.6	2.1	1.1	3.6	15.0	11.0	45	39
Islamic Development Bank	0.4	0.9	0.5	0.6	2.4	22.1	6.2	53	48
OPEC Fund	0.7	0.8	0.9	0.6	1.7	16.4	6.4	52	48
Other	6.1	3.1	8.4	2.2	1.7	19.6	5.6	50	48
IMF (SAF/ESAF/PRGF/Trust Fund)	3.7	8.9	5.0	6.4	0.5	10.0	5.5	52	32
Nonconcessional	167.8	293.2	100.0	100.0	5.7[4]	16.0[4]	3.9[4]	21[4]	10[4]
IBRD	27.7	118.9	16.5	40.6	6.3	14.7	4.8	22	6
IDB	10.0	37.2	6.0	12.7	6.1	13.3	4.1	18	6
AsDB	4.7	26.8	2.8	9.1	6.7	22.2	4.8	21	5
AfDB	4.1	9.3	2.4	3.2	7.3	17.8	4.8	63	2
European Investment Bank	1.9	8.8	1.1	3.0	4.6	15.9	4.5	32	26
BIS	0.0	3.2	0.0	1.1	. . .	. . .	. . .	. . .	. . .
EBRD	. . .	2.7	. . .	0.9	5.7	15.2	2.8	23	17
Corporación Andina de Fomento	0.0	1.6	0.0	0.5	7.2	8.4	2.4	9	−1
Central American Bank for Economic Integration	0	1.6	0.2	0.5	. . .	. . .	. . .	. . .	. . .
Council of Europe	0.5	1.4	0.3	0.5	5.6	10.0	6.0	9	−1
Nordic Investment Bank	0.2	1.0	0.1	0.3	. . .	. . .	. . .	. . .	. . .
Islamic Development Bank	0.1	0.6	0.0	0.2	2.4	2.3	0.4	7	6
Other	89.3	10.1	53.2	3.5	5.1	20.5	2.1	18	21
IMF (General Resources Account)	29.0	70.0	17.3	23.9	3.5	5.9	3.5	25	9

Sources: World Bank Debtor Reporting System (DRS) and *Global Development Finance* (GDF); OECD Press Releases; Annual Reports of the World Bank, AfDB/AfDF, AsDB, and IDB; and IMF staff estimates.

Note: Multilateral debt (including to the IMF) of a group of 137 countries reporting while World Bank estimates are used for the others. Major institution is defined as one with $0.5 billion or more debt outstanding at end-1999. Concessional debt is lending where grant element is at least 25 percent by OECD definition and is usually provided through special windows or funds within the lending institutions.

[1]Weighted by new commitments in reference year.

[2]For the purpose of calculating the grant element, loans are assumed to be repaid in equal semiannual installments of principal, and the grace period is defined as the interval to first repayment minus one payment period, or one semester, in this case.

[3]Commercial interest reference rates. For the World Bank and the main regional development banks (AfDB/AfDF, AsDB and IDB), the CIRR-based discount rate is derived from the average CIRRs in February–August 1999, weighted for the top five currencies in which the outstanding loans are repayable. For the other institutions, average CIRRs in 1999 for either the U.S. dollar, ECU/Euro, or SDR are used. For loans with an original maturity of 15 years or more, CIRRs averaged over the period 1990–99 are used. A margin reflecting longer repayment periods was added (0.75 percentage points for repayment period of less than 15 years, 1.0 percentage points for 15–20 years, 1.15 percentage points for 20–30 years, and 1.25 percentage points for over 30 years).

[4]Excluding IMF.

[5]IDA credits have maturities of 35 and 40 years with a 10-year grace period on repayment of principal. There is no interest charge, but credits do carry a small service charge, currently 0.75 percent on disbursed balances.

CHAPTER V

DEBT RESCHEDULING WITH OFFICIAL BILATERAL CREDITORS

Paris Club Reschedulings, August 1997–December 2000

Since August 1997, Paris Club creditors have concluded 40 rescheduling or deferral agreements, involving debt service obligations and arrears amounting to about $59 billion (Table 5.1). Among these agreements, 24 were concluded on highly concessional terms, while 16 agreements were reached on nonconcessional terms, mostly with middle-income countries.[23] Debt service payable after rescheduling represented about one-third of debt service falling due. In addition to flow and stock reschedulings, Paris Club creditors also agreed to a full or partial deferral of debt service obligations to six countries that were affected by conflict or natural disasters.

Paris Club creditors have continued to provide debt reduction to low-income countries through flow reschedulings and stock-of-debt operations. In addition to Naples terms (67 percent debt reduction in NPV terms on eligible debt in most cases), creditors have adopted more concessional rescheduling terms in the context of the HIPC Initiative of 1996 and its enhancement in 1999, involving debt reduction of up to 80 percent under the original HIPC Initiative (Lyon terms) and 90 percent under the enhanced Initiative (Cologne terms) (Table 5.2).[24] These efforts, and more broadly debt relief under the HIPC Initiative and additional voluntary bilateral debt cancellation, have substantially increased the prospects for low-income countries to exit from the rescheduling process and achieve sustainable external debt positions.

Most middle-income countries have graduated from rescheduling agreements with Paris Club creditors and some countries could do so at the end of their current rescheduling periods (Table 5.3). This reflects mainly the progress these countries made in stabilizing their economies, implementing structural reforms, and increasing their access to market financing.

Recent rescheduling agreements share a number of common features. The agreements typically covered medium- and long-term debt contracted before the cutoff date by the government or the public sector (or guaranteed by the government), but not amounts due under the most recent rescheduling. In cases of exceptional financing need, arrears on post-cutoff date or short-term debts could be deferred over a shorter period of time. The consolidation periods of flow rescheduling agreements typically covered the periods of IMF arrangements. All multiyear agreements included (typically three annual) tranches and trigger clauses that linked the effectiveness of the tranches to the existence of an appropriate arrangement with the IMF and a good payments record to creditors. All agreements contained a **comparability of treatment clause** requiring debtor countries to seek reschedulings from other official bilateral and commercial creditors on terms at least as favorable as those granted by the Paris Club.

In 2000, Paris Club creditors also agreed to expand voluntary debt swaps to a number of upper-middle-income countries. Previously debt swap provisions only figured in concessional rescheduling agreements with low-

---

[23]In general, the Paris Club grants concessional terms to countries that are only eligible for concessional assistance by the World Bank ("IDA-only countries"). Other countries usually receive nonconcessional terms. Creditors decide on the terms to be applied on a case-by-case basis.

[24]In November 2000, creditors decided to treat arrears on eligible debt accumulated by HIPCs before they reach their decision points on Naples terms (instead of Cologne terms) to discourage the accumulation of such arrears.

Table 5.1. Paris Club Reschedulings of Official Bilateral Debt, August 1997–December 2000

(In chronological order)

Debtor Countries	Number of Reschedulings[1]	Date of Agreement (Mo/Day/Yr)	Amount Consolidated[2] (Millions of U.S. dollars)	Type of Debt Consolidated[2,3] Not previously rescheduled	Previously rescheduled	Consoli- dation Period (Months)	Terms[4] Grace (Years)	Maturity (Years)
1997								
Cameroon[5]	V	10/24/97	1,350	PIA	Partial PIAL	35	Naples terms[6]	
Yemen, Republic of	II	11/20/97	1,446	Partial PIAL	—	36	Naples terms	
1998								
Nicaragua[5]	III	04/22/98	452	PIAL	Partial PIAL	36	Naples terms	
Côte d'Ivoire	VIII	04/24/98	1,332	PIAL	PIAL	36	Lyon terms	
Uganda	VII	04/24/98	148	—	Stock	—	Lyon terms	
Senegal	XII	06/17/98	590	Stock	Stock	—	Naples terms	
Albania	II TOR	07/22/98	75	AL	—	—	Naples terms[6]	
Rwanda	I	07/28/98	64	PIAL	—	34	Naples terms	
Indonesia[7]	I	09/23/98	4,176	P	—	20	3.0	10.0
Central African Rep.	VII	09/25/98	23	PIAL	PIAL	34	Naples terms	
Bosnia and Herzegovina[8]	I	10/28/98	674	PIAL	PIA	10	Naples terms	
Bolivia	VII	10/30/98	561	—	Stock	—	Lyon terms	
1999								
Pakistan[7]	I	01/30/99	3,250	PIA	—	24	3.0	18.0
Nicaragua[8]	III Amend.	03/16/99	448	—	PIAL	27	1.6	6.1
Honduras[9]	IV	04/13/99	411	PIAL	PIAL	36	Naples terms	
Zambia[5]	VII	04/16/99	1,060	PIA	Partial PIA	36	Naples terms	
Jordan	V	05/20/99	821	PIAL	Partial PIAL	37	3.0	18.0
Guyana	V	06/25/99	240	—	Stock	—	Lyon terms	
Mozambique	VI	07/09/99	1,860	—	Stock	—	90% NPV reduction	
Russian Federation	V	08/01/99	8,040	PIAL	Partial PIAL	18	1.4	20.0
Albania[8]	III TOR	10/14/99	89	PIAL	PIAL	15	1.1	5.6
2000								
Madagascar	VIII Amend. 1	01/13/00	23	PIAL	PIAL	12	Naples terms	
Mozambique[8]	VI Amend.	03/15/00	71	PIAL	—	12	0.2	4.7
Mauritania	VII	03/16/00	98	PIAL	PIAL	36	Cologne terms	
Djibouti	I TOR	03/22/00	17	PIAL	—	32	4.5	9.0
Indonesia	II	04/13/00	5,440	P	—	24	3.2	15.0
Tanzania[5]	VI	04/13/00	709	PIAL	PIAL	36	Cologne terms	
São Tomé and Príncipe	I	05/16/00	28	PIAL	—	37	Naples terms	
Bosnia and Herzegovina	I Amend.	07/28/00	9	PI	PI	12	Naples terms	
Madagascar[8]	VIII Amend. 2	08/18/00	34	PIAL	PIAL	6	1.5	8.0
Macedonia, FYR[8]	II TOR	09/01/00	46	PIAL	PIAL	12	1.0	5.5
Benin	V	09/12/00	5	—	PI	12	Cologne terms	
Uganda	VIII	09/12/00	145	—	Stock	—	Cologne terms	
Ecuador[5]	VII	09/15/00	804	PIAL	PI	12	3.0	18.0
Burkina Faso	IV	10/24/00	2	—	PI	12	Cologne terms	
Mali	V	10/24/00	4	—	PI	10	Cologne terms	
Senegal	XIII	10/24/00	21	—	PI	18	Cologne terms	
Kenya	II	11/15/00	302	PIA	PIA	12	3.0	20.0
Nigeria[5]	IV	12/13/00	23,380	PI	PI	12	3.0	18.0
Gabon[5]	VIII	12/15/00	687	PIA	PIA	n.a.	3.3	12.0

Sources: Agreed Minutes of debt reschedulings; Paris Club Secretariat; and IMF staff estimates.

[1]Roman numerals indicate, for each country, the number of debt reschedulings in the period beginning 1976.

[2]Includes debt service formally rescheduled as well as deferred.

[3]Key: P – Principal; I – Interest; A – Arrears on principal and interest; L – Late interest. P, I, and A are on pre-cutoff date medium- and long-term debt.

[4]Terms for rescheduled debt, calculated from the midpoint of the consolidation period plus 6 months; terms for deferred amounts, if any, tend to be shorter.

[5]Agreement featured an entry-into-force clause.

[6]Naples terms with a 50 percent NPV reduction.

[7]Rescheduling with the Group of Participating Creditor Countries.

[8]Nonconcessional deferral.

[9]The agreement included a deferral of all the remaining payments due during the consolidation period.

Table 5.2. Evolution of Paris Club Rescheduling Terms

	Lower-Middle-Income		Toronto terms options			London Terms[3] Options				Low-Income Countries[2] — Naples Terms Options[4]					Lyon terms[5] options				Cologne terms options[5,6]
	Middle-Income Countries[1]	Countries (Houston terms)[1]	DR	DSR	LM	DR	DSR	CMI	LM	DR	DSR Maturing flows	DSR Stocks	CMI	LM	DR	DSR	CMI	LM	DR
Implemented	...	Since Sept. 1990	Oct. 1988–June 1991			Dec. 1991–Dec. 1994				Since January 1995					Dec. 1996–Oct. 1999				Since Nov. 1999
Grace (in years)	5–6[1]	Up to 8[1]	8	8	14	6	—	5	16[7]	6	—	3	8	20	6	8	8	20	6
Maturity (in years)	9[1]	15[1]	14	14	25	23	23	23	25	23	33	33	33	40	23	40	40	40	23
Repayment schedule	Flat/ graduated	Flat/ graduated	Flat ———→			Graduated ———→				Graduated ———→					Graduated ———→				Graduated
Interest rate[8]	M	M	M	R[9]	M	M	R[10]	R[10]	M	M	R[11]	R[11]	R[11]	M	M	R[11]	R[12]	M	M
Reduction in net present value (in percent)	—	—	33	20–30[13]	—	50	50	50	—	67	67	67	67	—	80	80	80	—	90[6]
Memorandum items																			
ODA creditsGrace (in years)	5–6	Up to 10	12	14	14	12	12	12	16	16	16	16	16	20	16	16	16	20	16
Maturity (in years)	10	20	25	25	25	30	30	30	25	40	40	40	40	40	40	40	40	40	40

Source: Paris Club.

[1]Since the 1992 agreements with Argentina and Brazil, creditors have made increasing use of graduated payments schedules (up to 15 years' maturity and 2–3 years' grace for middle-income countries; up to 18 years' maturity for lower-middle-income countries).

[2]DR refers to the debt-reduction option; DRS to the debt-service-reduction option; CMI denotes the capitalization of moratorium interest; LM denotes the nonconcessional option providing longer maturities. Under London, Naples, Lyon, and Cologne terms, there is a provision for a stock-of-debt operation, but no such operation took place under London terms.

[3]These have also been called "Enhanced Toronto" and "Enhanced Concessions" terms.

[4]Until November 1999 included an option of a 50 percent level of concessionality for countries with a per capita income of more than $500, and an overall net present value of debt/export ratio of less than 350 percent. For a 50 percent level of concessionality, terms were equal to London terms except for the debt-service-reduction option under a stock-of-debt operation that included a three-year grace period.

[5]These terms are to be granted in the context of concerted action by all creditors under the HIPC Initiative. They also include, on a voluntary basis, an ODA debt-reduction option.

[6]Creditors agree on a case-by-case basis on a net present value debt reduction of 90 percent on pre-cutoff date commercial (non-ODA) debt, or more if this is required in the context of proportional burden sharing with other creditors to achieve debt sustainability in the debtor country. All creditors will seek to apply the DR option, but if that is not possible there is also a DSR option with very long maturities and grace periods.

[7]Fourteen years before June 1992.

[8]Interest rates are determined in the bilateral agreements implementing the Paris Club Agreed Minute. M = market rates. M = market rates; R = reduced rates.

[9]The interest rate was 3.5 percentage points below the market rate or half of the market rate if the market rate was below 7 percent.

[10]Reduced to achieve a 50 percent net present value reduction.

[11]Reduced to achieve a 67 percent net present value reduction; under the DSR option for the stock operation, the interest rate is slightly higher, reflecting the three-year grace period.

[12]Reduced to achieve an 80 percent net present value reduction.

[13]The reduction of net present value depends on the reduction in interest rates and therefore varies. See Footnote 9.

income and lower-middle-income countries.[25] For a number of years Paris Club creditors have engaged in debt swaps (see Appendix VI) with low-income and some lower-middle-income countries. There are no limits on swaps involving ODA debt, and limits on swaps of non-ODA claims are set case-by-case in the rescheduling agreements. As of end-2000, swap requests of three upper-middle-income countries had been granted: Algeria, Bulgaria, and Morocco. Creditors are to report semi-annually on all debt swap operations they have implemented.

Rescheduling Agreements on Middle-Income Terms[26]

There have been 11 flow rescheduling or deferral agreements on middle-income terms since mid-1997.[27] Coverage and conditions of the rescheduling agreements varied, depending on the financing needs of the debtor country. All agreements involved graduated payments for commercial debt and flat payments on ODA debt.

In September 1998 and April 2000, **Indonesia** and Paris Club creditors agreed on a rescheduling of principal maturities on pre-cutoff date (July 1, 1997) medium- and long-term government and government-guaranteed debt falling due during August 1998–March 2000 and during April 2000–March 2002 over 10–11 years, including 3–4 years' grace. The entry-into-force of the 2000 agreement was linked to the completion by the IMF Board of the first review under the EFF arrangement, which took place in June 2000.

Pakistan agreed with the Paris Club in January 1999 on a rescheduling of arrears (excluding late interest) and current maturities on pre-

cutoff date (September 30, 1997) debt of the public sector falling due through end-2000. Commercial debt was rescheduled over 18 years with 3 years' grace (Houston terms), while ODA debts were rescheduled over 20 years, including 10 years' grace. The Pakistani government committed itself to seek from bondholders the reorganization of bonds on terms comparable to Paris Club terms, and undertook a highly successful bond exchange offer in November 1999.

In April 1999, Paris Club creditors granted to **the former Yugoslav Republic of Macedonia** a deferral of all arrears and current maturities due during the following year over a 5½ year period, including 1 year of grace, in order to mitigate the effects of the Kosovo crisis; a similar deferral was granted to Albania (see below).

An agreement with **Jordan** in May 1999 covered arrears[28] and current maturities falling due through April 2002 on pre-cutoff date (January 1, 1989) medium- and long-term debt of the public sector, except for debt falling due under the last rescheduling agreement (1997). The rescheduling agreement involved maturities of 18 years for commercial debt, including grace periods of 3 years, while ODA debts were rescheduled over 20 years, including grace periods of 10 years.

In August 1999, **Russia** and Paris Club creditors agreed on a flow rescheduling on certain arrears and current maturities falling due through December 2000 on its Soviet-era public sector debt. Most of the previously rescheduled debt was rescheduled over 16 years, including 1½ years' grace;[29] payments due on short-term debt and post-cutoff date debt contracted in 1991 were deferred over six years, including one year of grace. This agreement included a goodwill clause under which creditors indicated their willingness to discuss comprehensive solu-

---

[25]With a view to ensuring the transparency of the swap agreements, creditors will be required to inform the Secretariat of the Paris Club of their intention to implement debt swap agreements with upper-middle-income countries.

[26]Nonconcessional terms as defined in Table 5.2.

[27]Excluding the nonconcessional deferrals granted to Albania, Honduras, Madagascar, Mozambique, and Nicaragua, which are discussed below.

[28]Excluding a small amount of arrears on the 1994 rescheduling agreement.

[29]Twenty years for not previously scheduled debt.

Table 5.3. Status of Paris Club Rescheduling Countries as of End-December 2000

Low-Income[1]		Lower-Middle-Income[2]		Other Middle-Income		Total
Countries that graduated from reschedulings[3]						
** Albania	6/00[8]	Dominican Republic	12/99	Algeria	5/98	
** Bosnia/Herzegovina	4/00	Egypt	5/91	Argentina	3/95	
** Cambodia	6/97	El Salvador	9/91	Bulgaria	4/95	
** Haiti	3/96	Ghana	4/96[4, 5]	Brazil	8/93	
**** Uganda	9/00	Guatemala	3/93	Chile	12/88	
* Vietnam	12/93[4]	Jamaica	9/95[4, 6]	Costa Rica	6/93[4]	
		Morocco	12/92	Croatia	12/95	
		Peru	12/98[7]	Macedonia, FYR	3/00[8]	
		Philippines	7/94[9]	Mexico	5/92	
		Pakistan	12/00	Panama	3/92	
		Poland	4/91	Romania	12/83	
				Russian Federation	12/00	
				Trinidad and Tobago	3/91	
				Turkey	6/83	
Number of countries	**6**		**11**		**14**	**31**
Countries with rescheduling agreements in effect						
**** Benin	6/01	Djibouti	6/02			
**** Burkina Faso	6/01	Ecuador	4/01			
** Central African Republic, The	6/01	Gabon	12/00[4]			
*** Côte d'Ivoire	8/01	Indonesia	3/02			
** Honduras	3/02[8]	Jordan	4/02			
**** Mali	6/01	Kenya	6/01			
**** Mauritania	6/02	Nigeria	7/01			
*** Mozambique	6/01[8]					
** Nicaragua	2/01[8]					
** Rwanda	5/01					
** São Tomé and Príncipe	4/03					
**** Senegal	12/01					
**** Tanzania	3/03					
** Zambia	3/02					
Number of countries	**14**		**7**		**0**	**21**

tions to Russia's Soviet-era debt; discussions on this were to begin in the fall of 2000, but have not commenced because of Russia's much improved balance-of-payments situation and the absence of an IMF arrangement.

In September 2000, **Ecuador** and Paris Club creditors agreed on a flow rescheduling of medium- and long-term pre-cutoff date (July 28, 1983) arrears and maturities on debt of the public sector falling due during May 2000–April 2001 on terms similar to those received by Pakistan. In addition, most of the late interest on pre-cutoff date debt as well as post-cutoff date arrears were deferred over five years. The agreement with Ecuador included a goodwill clause, under which the creditors committed themselves in principle to consider a further rescheduling of Ecuador's debt falling due after April 30, 2001.

In December 2000, agreement was reached with **Nigeria** on the rescheduling of arrears (including late interest) and maturities on medium- and long-term pre-cutoff date (October 1, 1985) debt of the public sector falling due during August 2000–July 2001. The rescheduled amounts were to be repaid over 18 years, includ-

Table 5.3 *(concluded)*

	Low-Income[1]	Lower-Middle-Income[2]	Other Middle-Income	Total
	Countries with previous rescheduling agreements, but without current rescheduling agreements, which have not graduated from reschedulings			
Angola	9/90		Yugoslavia, FR[11] 6/89	
*** Bolivia	10/98			
** Cameroon	8/00[10]			
** Chad	8/98			
Congo, Democratic Republic of	6/90[12]			
* Equatorial Guinea	2/96			
Gambia, The	9/87			
** Guinea	12/00[10]			
** Guinea-Bissau	6/98			
*** Guyana	6/99			
Liberia	6/85			
** Madagascar	11/00[8]			
Malawi	5/89			
** Niger	6/99			
** Sierra Leone	12/97			
Somalia	12/88			
Sudan	12/84			
** Togo	6/98			
** Yemen, Republic of	10/00			
Number of countries	**19**	**0**	**1**	**20**
All countries	**39**	**18**	**15**	**72**

Sources: Paris Club Secretariat; and Fund staff estimates.

Note: Stock treatment underlined. Dates refer to end of current or last consolidation period. In the case of a stock-of-debt operation, canceled agreements, or rescheduling of arrears only, date shown is that of relevant agreement.

[1]* denotes rescheduling on London terms, **denotes rescheduling on Naples terms, *** denotes rescheduling on Lyon terms, and ****denotes rescheduling on Cologne terms. Several "graduated" countries, including with previous debt stock reschedulings, are expected to require a new rescheduling on Cologne terms in the context of the HIPC Initiative.

[2]Defined here as countries that obtained lower-middle-income but not concessional terms with Paris Club reschedulings.

[3]For some countries, this inevitably represents an element of judgment: in certain circumstances, for example, if hit by an external shock, a country may need further reschedulings.

[4]Rescheduling of arrears only.

[5]Limited deferral of long-standing arrears to three creditors on nonconcessional terms.

[6]Nonconcessional rescheduling at the authorities' request.

[7]Agreement includes a reprofiling of the stock of certain debts at the end of the consolidation period.

[8]Including deferral of maturities.

[9]The 1994 rescheduling agreement was canceled at the authorities' request.

[10]Involved debt relief of 50 percent in NPV terms.

[11]Former Socialist Federal Republic of Yugoslavia.

[12]Last rescheduling on Toronto terms.

ing 3 years' grace for commercial debt, and 20 years, including 10 years of grace for ODA debt. Part of the arrears were reorganized over 9 years and allocated to creditors in order to bring all of them to a level of payments of about one-fourth of the amounts due to them since the last rescheduling in 1991. In addition, moratorium interest on the rescheduling was fully capitalized and deferred over five years, including two years of grace. Arrears on post-cutoff date debt were deferred over five years as well. The agreement included a goodwill clause, under which creditors agreed in principle to consider possible op-

tions in further restructuring Nigeria's debt falling due after July 31, 2001.

During the same month, creditors also reached agreement with **Gabon** on the rescheduling of arrears on pre-cutoff date (July 1, 1986) medium- and long-term government (and government-guaranteed) debt over 12 years, including 3 years of grace. The rescheduling excluded arrears on debt rescheduled under the 1995 Paris Club agreement. Late interest was deferred over two years, while arrears on the 1995 agreement as well as arrears on post-cutoff date debt were deferred until 2001. The agreement also included a debt swap clause.

There were two reschedulings with low-income countries on nonconcessional terms. In March 2000, **Djibouti** received a nonconcessional rescheduling of arrears (including late interest) and maturities on pre-cutoff date debt (March 31, 1998) falling due during March 2000–January 2003. The consolidated amounts were deferred over 10 years, including 6 years of grace.

In November 2000, **Kenya** obtained a nonconcessional rescheduling (Houston terms with 18 years maturity, including 3 years of grace) of pre-cutoff date (December 12, 1991) debt that had not been rescheduled before, covering arrears (excluding late interest) and current maturities falling due during July 2000–June 2001. Arrears on the 1994 rescheduling agreement were not included in the consolidation, but deferred until end-June 2001.

Rescheduling Agreements on Low-Income Country Terms[30]

In the period August 1997–December 2000, Paris Club creditors reached 25 agreements on flow reschedulings and stock-of-debt operations on concessional terms with low-income countries (including amendments). Of those, 12 agreements were related to the implementation of the HIPC Initiative. In addition, creditors reached agreement with five low-income countries on deferrals related to conflicts or natural disasters.

In November 1999, the Paris Club reached agreement on new terms with a higher degree of concessionality for countries that have reached their decision points under the enhanced HIPC Initiative (Cologne terms). As interim assistance during the period between the decision point and the completion point under the enhanced Initiative, the Paris Club provides Cologne flow reschedulings with a 90 percent reduction in NPV terms on eligible debt and coverage tailored on a case-by-case basis. At the completion point, creditors will provide irrevocable debt reduction as required under the principle of proportional burden sharing.

The Paris Club agreements related to the implementation of the HIPC Initiative were on Lyon terms under the original HIPC framework, or on Cologne terms under the enhanced framework. These included a Lyon flow rescheduling for Côte d'Ivoire, the topping up of the 1995/96 stock-of-debt operations from Naples to Lyon (80 percent NPV reduction) terms for Uganda, Bolivia, and Guyana, as well as Cologne flow reschedulings for Mauritania and Tanzania. In addition, current debt service due previously rescheduled on Naples terms for Benin, Burkina Faso, Mali, and Senegal was topped up to a 90 percent reduction in NPV terms. As of end-December 2000, Paris Club creditors have indicated their willingness to grant additional debt relief through topping up to three other countries that had achieved their decision points under the enhanced HIPC Initiative (Nicaragua, São Tomé and Príncipe, and Zambia). Uganda's stock operation was topped up from Lyon to Cologne terms after it had reached the completion point under the enhanced HIPC Initiative in May 2000. Mozambique received a 90 percent debt reduction in NPV terms in the context of a stock-of-debt operation agreed in principle in July 1999, after the country reached its completion point under the original Initiative.

Agreements for other low-income countries included 11 flow reschedulings and one stock-of-debt operation (Senegal) on Naples terms and 5 deferrals. The agreements with Albania (1998) and Cameroon were with a 50 percent NPV reduction, others with a 67 percent NPV reduction on eligible debt: Bosnia/Herzegovina (1998 and 2000), the Central African Republic, Honduras, Nicaragua, Rwanda, São Tomé and Príncipe, Yemen, and Zambia.

[30]As defined in Table 5.2.

The coverage of the agreements was comprehensive. In all flow rescheduling agreements, current maturities[31] and arrears[32] on pre-cutoff date medium- and long-term debts (except debt service obligations on the most recent Paris Club rescheduling), not previously rescheduled (NPRD) or rescheduled nonconcessionally, were consolidated. Obligations received Naples, Lyon, or Cologne terms, and obligations due under previous non- or less-concessional rescheduling agreements were typically topped up to the concessionality level being provided in the latest agreement.[33]

In cases of exceptional financing need, Paris Club creditors agreed also to treat on nonconcessional terms some debt service obligations that are normally not treated: payments due on the most recent rescheduling, moratorium interest on the current agreement, and arrears or current maturities on short-term debt and post-cutoff date debt. **Bosnia-Herzegovina** received a nonconcessional deferral of short-term debt in arrears (including late interest) or due during the consolidation period. For the **Central African Republic**, the amounts due under the consolidation agreements of 1988 and 1990 that had been deferred nonconcessionally were topped up to Naples terms. The agreement with **Cameroon** provided for the deferral of arrears (including late interest) and current ma-

turities on London and Naples terms debt falling due during the period from mid-October 1997 through June 1998, while arrears (including late interest) and current maturities of the interest obligations reprofiled in the 1994 and 1995 reschedulings were again reprofiled.[34] In the case of **Côte d'Ivoire,** late interest, arrears (excluding late interest), and current maturities falling due on London terms debt were deferred.[35] The flow reschedulings (on Cologne terms) for **Mauritania** and **Tanzania** were very comprehensive and included maturities falling due under the most recent rescheduling in anticipation of the broad coverage and high levels of debt reduction required under the HIPC Initiative.[36] Finally, for **Zambia**, large amounts of arrears and current maturities on post-cutoff date debt due to Russia were deferred.[37]

In response to exceptional circumstances, Paris Club creditors provided comprehensive deferrals to five low-income countries. To help overcome the economic difficulties caused by hurricane Mitch in late 1998, the Paris Club deferred on nonconcessional terms all debt service obligations (including payments on short-term debt and post-cutoff date debt) of **Honduras** due between end-October 1998 and end-March 2002 and of **Nicaragua** due between end-November 1998 and end-February 2001; the deferred

[31]Except in the case of Yemen where, in line with the declining financing needs of the IMF-supported program, Paris Club creditors in the third year of the program rescheduled only the interest falling due on not previously rescheduled debt (July 1999 to October 2000).

[32]Including late interest for Bosnia, the Central African Republic, Honduras, Nicaragua, Rwanda, and Yemen. In the case of Côte d'Ivoire, late interest (including on debt previously rescheduled concessionally) was deferred nonconcessionally, and was to be paid in five equal semiannual installments from March 1999 to March 2001.

[33]In the case of Honduras, this implied the topping-up of PRD on Naples terms with a 50 percent NPV reduction to a 67 percent NPV reduction. For Cameroon, the PRD on London terms was not topped up since the level of concessionality of the new agreement (50 percent NPV reduction) was the same as the concessionality provided under the previous rescheduling agreement.

[34]Principal and interest falling due during the period October 1997–June 1998. All principal and interest falling due during the subsequent two years of the consolidation period were to be paid as scheduled. Seventy percent of the amounts deferred were to be paid by end-June 1999, and the remaining 30 percent by end-June 2000. The terms of the reprofiling were: 3-year maturity, including one-year grace period.

[35]Arrears: 5-year maturity, including 1½ years' grace; current maturities: 15-year maturity, including 3 years' grace.

[36]In the case of Tanzania, arrears accrued since the end of the consolidation period (November 1999) of the previous rescheduling agreement were exempt. In a side letter the Japanese authorities agreed to a deferral over three years of maturities under the 1997 rescheduling in light of the continuing delays in signing the related bilateral agreement.

[37]Over 10 years, including 5 years' grace.

amounts were to be repaid over five years, including one year's grace.

To ease the balance of payments pressures caused by the Kosovo crisis in 1999, **Albania** was granted a nonconcessional deferral of arrears (including late interest) and current medium- and long-term maturities due between end-March 1999 and end-June 2000. As in the case of the Former Yugoslav Republic of Macedonia, the repayment terms provided for a maturity of 5½ years, including a grace period of about 1 year.

Following serious floods and the displacement of more than one million people in early 2000, **Mozambique** received a nonconcessional deferral of payments due (including short-term debt) from February 1, 2000, up to the date of the approval by the Boards of the Fund and the World Bank of the completion point under the enhanced HIPC Initiative (or end-June 2001, if this date is earlier). The agreement envisaged a repayment period of five years, with no grace. Finally, in light of the heavy damage caused by tornados in 2000, **Madagascar** received a nonconcessional deferral of payments falling due between July 1 and end-November 2000 (excluding a part of debt service obligations on post-cutoff date debt), with repayments over 5½ years (including 1 year of grace).

The coverage of the stock-of-debt operations was also comprehensive. In 1998 **Senegal** received a 67 percent debt reduction in NPV terms on principal and interest arrears (excluding late interest) on medium- and long-term pre-cutoff date (January 1, 1983) debt, including a topping up of debt previously rescheduled on Toronto and London terms and debt nonconcessionally deferred under the 1994 agreement. Small amounts falling due on debt rescheduled in 1989, 1990, and 1991 (Toronto terms) that were deferred nonconcessionally in 1995 were deferred again nonconcessionally.[38]

When the Paris Club topped up **Uganda**'s 1995 stock-of-debt operation from Naples to Lyon terms in April 1998, creditors broadened the coverage by also topping up the debt rescheduled in 1992 but not treated in 1995, and debt deferred nonconcessionally in 1992. An agreement was reached with **Bolivia** in September 1998 to top up earlier debt relief from Naples terms to Lyon terms. This covered 84 percent of the pre-cutoff date debt rescheduled under both the March 1995 flow rescheduling and the December 1995 stock-of-debt operation. In June 1999, 65 percent of **Guyana**'s stock of pre-cutoff date medium- and long-term public debt was topped up from 67 to 80 percent NPV reduction, in line with the Paris Club's proportional cost share in HIPC Initiative assistance. In July 1999, all of **Mozambique**'s stock of pre-cutoff date medium- and long-term debt was rescheduled with a 90 percent debt reduction in NPV terms. All of these stock agreements are expected to be topped up to Cologne terms when these countries reach their completion points under the enhanced HIPC Initiative, as was done for Uganda in September 2000.[39]

All agreements with low-income countries included *debt swap clauses*. These allow creditors to sell or exchange on a voluntary basis part of their commercial claims (and all of their ODA claims) in the framework of debt-for-nature, debt-for-aid, debt-for-equity swaps or other local currency debt swaps (for more information on debt swaps see Appendix VI).

The agreements for Cameroon, Nicaragua, Tanzania, and Zambia included entry-into-force clauses that linked the coming into force of the rescheduling agreement to the receipt by creditors of certain payments (normally arrears not covered by the agreement). In the case of **Nicaragua**, this included payments due to three creditors resulting from the retroactive imple-

---

[38]Over 11 years, including one-year grace, with semiannual graduated payments.
[39]As the outstanding stock of pre-cutoff date debt was smaller than the amount of HIPC Initiative assistance to be provided by the Paris Club, the stock-of-debt operation for Uganda also covered post-cutoff date debt.

mentation of the second and third tranches of the 1995 rescheduling agreement.[40] The entry-into-force of the agreement with **Cameroon** was conditional on the payment of arrears on short-term debt deferred under previous rescheduling agreements. The agreement with **Zambia** became effective only after the payment of late interest and arrears on amounts not consolidated. The January 1997 agreement with **Tanzania** entered into force with an 18-month delay after Tanzania cleared arrears to a de minimis creditor.

All flow rescheduling agreements for low-income countries contained a goodwill clause. Under this clause, creditors indicated their willingness to **consider a stock-of-debt operation** at the end of the consolidation period, if the country continued to have an appropriate arrangement with the IMF and had fully implemented the rescheduling agreement. The agreements for Côte d'Ivoire, Nicaragua, and Rwanda also included a **HIPC clause**, indicating creditors' willingness to consider possible debt relief under the HIPC Initiative. Also, in the context of **HIPC Initiative decision points**, Paris Club creditors indicated their willingness to provide a stock-of-debt operation at the completion point.

Recent Debt Restructurings with Non-Paris Club Bilateral Creditors

Countries that reschedule debt with Paris Club creditors typically also have debts to other official bilateral and private commercial creditors on which they need to seek comparable treatment. Agreements with the Paris Club include provisions requiring these debtors to seek relief from the non-Paris Club bilateral creditors on terms at least as favorable to the debtor as those granted by Paris Club creditors. In practice, such comparable treatment is often not provided, and arrears accumulate instead.

Reflecting the absence of an established institutional forum for debtor negotiations with non-Paris Club creditors, debt restructurings among this group of bilateral creditors have taken a number of forms. Information on such restructuring agreements is not, however, readily available from a centralized source. A summary of bilateral debt restructurings involving non-Paris Club creditors is provided in Table 5.4.

During 1997–99, bilateral debt restructurings by official non-Paris Club creditors have generally taken one of three forms. The **first**, and most common form, has been the rescheduling of principal and interest repayments on concessional or nonconcessional terms. This has been the case for the debt restructuring agreements in the following cases: Brazil and Bolivia; Kyrgyz Republic and Tajikistan; Kuwait and Comoros; North Korea and Equatorial Guinea; Turkey and Tajikistan; and Uzbekistan and Tajikistan.

A **second** common form of debt restructuring has been the use of debt buyback operations, covering a large share of the outstanding debt. A debt buyback operation took place with an 84 percent discount in the case of Argentina and Benin; an 86 percent discount in the case of Argentina and Guinea; an 89 percent discount in the case of the Czech Republic's claims on both Guinea and Zambia; and an 85 percent discount in the case of Tanzania and Uganda.

A **third** form of debt restructuring has involved the full or partial forgiveness of debt stocks through bilateral agreements. Argentina has forgiven 70 percent of its claims on Equatorial Guinea; Egypt has agreed to a 90 percent NPV reduction of its claims on Tanzania; and the Slovak Republic has provided 90 percent reduction in debt owed by Nicaragua. Other countries have gone even further, as in the case of Morocco, which has fully written off the debt owed by Mauritania (and pledged similar action for debt owed by Guinea); Venezuela, which offered 100 percent forgiveness on debt

---

[40]Nicaragua had serviced the debt rescheduled in the 1995 agreement to all but three creditors as if the second and third tranches had been implemented.

Table 5.4. Non-Paris Club Rescheduling of Official Bilateral Debt, 1997–2000

Creditor	Debtor	Agreement Date	Total Amount (US$ million)	Coverage[1]	Terms and Other Comments
Argentina	Benin	Jun–98	20.5	P	Buyback with 84 percent discount
Argentina	Equatorial Guinea	Mar–97	14.3	A+P	70 percent forgiven
Argentina	Guinea	Dec–98	22.5	P	Buyback with 86 percent discount
Brazil	Bolivia	Jan–00[2]	. . .	P+I	Rescheduling of outstanding obligations on terms comparable to Paris Club agreement
China	African HIPCs	. . .	1,200.0	A+P	Full debt write-off pledged to 16 African HIPCs in October 2000
Costa Rica	Nicaragua	. . .	383.0[3]	A+P	Creditor agreed in principle to deliver HIPC assistance
Czech Republic	Guinea	Oct–97	20.0	A	Buyback with 88.5 percent discount; payment in local (Guinean) currency
Czech Republic	Zambia	Nov–00	0.1[3]	P	Buyback with 89 percent discount
Egypt	Tanzania	Jul–00	0.4[3]	P	Creditor agreed to a 90 percent NPV reduction of outstanding debt
Guatemala	Nicaragua	. . .	364.0[3]	A+P	Creditor agreed in principle to deliver HIPC assistance
Honduras	Nicaragua	. . .	100.0[3]	A+P	Creditor agreed to deliver HIPC assistance
Kyrgyz Republic	Tajikistan	May–98	2.3	A	9-year maturity, 1-year of grace, 2.8 percent interest
Kuwait	Comoros	Jun–97[2]	4.0	A	Rescheduled over 18 years
Morocco	Mauritania	prior to Jan–00	. . .	P	Full debt write-off granted by creditor
Morocco	Guinea	. . .	24.7[3]	A+P	Creditor agreed in principle to forgive outstanding claims
Pakistan	Uganda	. . .	3.2	A+P	Creditor agreed in principle to deliver HIPC assistance
Pakistan	Guinea-Bissau	. . .	3.0	A+P	Creditor agreed in principle to deliver HIPC assistance
North Korea	Equatorial Guinea	Jul–97	1.2	A	Repayment over 2 years with no grace, zero interest
Poland	Bolivia	Jul–97	1.5	P	Upfront payment of 18 percent
Slovak Republic	Nicaragua	Apr–00	81.1	P	90 percent upfront reduction; remaining $8 million to be repaid over 13 years
South Africa	Mozambique	Mar–00[2]	2.0	P	Full debt write-off granted by creditor
Tanzania	Uganda	Aug–97	122.5	A	Buyback with 85 percent discount; US$ 58.1 million of the total is pending verification
Turkey	Tajikistan	Jan–98	25.7	A	Rescheduled with 13-year maturity, 3-year of grace, 2.8 percent interest
Uzbekistan	Tajikistan	Jan–98	151.0	PRD	Rescheduled with 13-year maturity, 3-year of grace, 2.8 percent interest
Venezuela	Bolivia	Jun–97	4.0	P	100 percent forgiven

Sources: Country authorities and IMF staff estimates.
[1]A = arrears; P = principal; I = interest; PRD = previously rescheduled debt.
[2]Approximate date.
[3]Amounts in net present value terms.
[4]Rescheduling took place in 1996.

owed by Bolivia; and South Africa, which has fully forgiven debt owed by Mozambique. In addition, China has recently pledged to forgive all debt owed by 16 African HIPCs.

Non-Paris Club creditors are expected to deliver their share of assistance under the HIPC Initiative based on the principle of proportional burden sharing. In this regard, notable decisions to participate in the HIPC Initiative have been taken by Costa Rica, Guatemala, and Honduras, who have all recently agreed to deliver their share of assistance to Nicaragua under the HIPC Initiative, and thus enabled Nicaragua to reach its enhanced decision point.

DEBT RESCHEDULING UNDER THE PARIS CLUB—A PRIMER

The Paris Club is an informal group of creditor governments mainly from industrialized countries that has met regularly in Paris since 1956 to reschedule bilateral debts; the French treasury provides the secretariat. Meetings generally take place every 4–6 weeks. Creditors meet with a debtor country to reschedule its debts as part of the international support provided to a country that is experiencing debt-servicing difficulties and is pursuing an adjustment program supported by the IMF. The Paris Club does not have a fixed membership, and its meetings are open to all official creditors that accept its practices and procedures. The core creditors are mainly OECD member countries, but other creditors attend as relevant for a debtor country.[41] Russia became a participating creditor in September 1997.

Paris Club creditors agree in a multilateral framework with debtor countries on the terms of a rescheduling, which are documented in the "Agreed Minute."[42] The terms of the rescheduling vary according to the debtor countries' circumstances and income level. The debtor then negotiates bilateral agreements with each creditor country based on the terms of the Agreed Minute. The framework provided by the Paris Club has greatly facilitated central negotiations on the rescheduling of bilateral debt, and has led to the standardization of rescheduling terms, especially for the low-income debtor countries. Notwithstanding this, the Club has preserved great flexibility in its functioning.

In recent years, the number of countries rescheduling with Paris Club creditors has declined. This mainly reflects the graduation from rescheduling of most middle-income countries as a result of the implementation of economic reforms that have increased their access to market financing. However, following the Asian crisis, a number of middle-income countries have required new reschedulings of their external debt. For example, Indonesia reached a rescheduling agreement in September 1998, and Pakistan in January 1999.

Also, low-income countries have begun to graduate from the rescheduling process. This reflects in part increasingly concessional and more comprehensive rescheduling terms granted by the Paris Club and the implementation of agreements to reduce debt stocks of low-income countries. With the further reduction of debt to sustainable levels reflecting assistance provided under the HIPC Initiative, it is expected that more low-income countries will graduate from the rescheduling process.

Principles of the Paris Club

Historically the Club's practices and procedures have not been documented in a formal way, but five key operating principles were spelled out for the first time in September 1997 in the context of Russia's participation in the Club as a creditor:

- *Consensus:* No decision can be reached in the Paris Club unless it is accepted by all participating creditor countries.
- *Solidarity among creditors:* No creditor will seek better treatment from a debtor country than that available to other Paris Club credi-

[41]A number of developing country creditors have participated in individual cases (for example, Brazil as a creditor for Mozambique and Guinea-Bissau). These countries include some Middle Eastern countries and some countries in the Western Hemisphere.

[42]If the number of participating creditors is small (not more than three), no rescheduling meeting takes place, but creditors present their offer to the debtor in the form of "Terms of Reference."

tors. As a consequence, no bilateral agreement can be negotiated between a participating creditor country and a debtor country if an appropriate Agreed Minute or Terms of Reference has not been previously concluded between the Paris Club and the debtor country concerned.

- *Conditionality:* The Paris Club will only reschedule debt of a debtor country that has a current program supported by an appropriate arrangement in the upper credit tranches with the IMF.

- *Comparability of treatment:* A participating creditor country, as well as any bilateral creditor not participating in the Paris Club, should never grant to a debtor country a treatment less favorable than provided for in the multilateral agreement with the Paris Club.

- *Case-by-case action:* Any decision taken in the Paris Club concerning the treatment of a debtor country's debt should be based on a specific assessment of the economic and financial situation of the country concerned and on a realistic approach.

Preconditions and Costs/Benefits

Official creditors at the Paris Club normally require two preconditions for the initiation of a debt rescheduling negotiation. First, the creditors must be convinced that the debtor country would be unable to meet its external payments obligations unless it receives debt relief; the country must demonstrate a **financing need**. Second, Paris Club creditors also insist that a debtor country seeking a rescheduling take the steps necessary to eliminate the causes of its payments difficulties in order to achieve a durable improvement in its external payments position. The debtor is therefore expected to undertake an **adjustment effort** in the context of an adjustment program supported by an upper credit tranche arrangement with the IMF.[43]

When a debtor country is considering whether to request a Paris Club rescheduling for the first time, trade-offs between the potential cost and the benefit should be assessed particularly carefully. A Paris Club rescheduling is likely to have a negative effect on a country's creditworthiness and access to new financing from export credit agencies, for example, that could be significant and difficult to repair. The immediate reaction of official export credit agencies might be to go "off cover"[44] not only for medium- and long-term loans, but also on short-term loans, or creditors might suspend or slow down disbursements from existing loan commitments. The potential impact on the volume and cost of new financing flows and on access to private capital markets would have to be weighed against the possible cash-flow relief of a rescheduling and, for concessional reschedulings, the NPV[45] reduction that might be expected.

The Modus Operandi of the Paris Club
Terms

The terms of a Paris Club rescheduling typically depend on the income level of the debtor country, as well as the category of debt involved (commercial debt with market-related interest rates, or ODA debt on concessional terms).[46]

---

[43]Upper credit tranche arrangements include Stand-By Arrangements, arrangements under the Poverty Reduction and Growth Facility and Extended Fund Facility and, for countries in arrears to the IMF, Rights Accumulation Programs.

[44]That is to stop providing export credit guarantees or insurance against risks of payment delays or nonpayments relating to export transactions.

[45]The discounted sum of all future debt service obligations (interest and principal) on existing debt. Whenever the interest rate on a loan is lower than the discount rate, the resulting NPV of debt is smaller than its face value, with the difference reflecting the grant element. The discount rates used in the context of the HIPC Initiative reflect market interest rates.

[46]The Paris Club uses the OECD/DAC definition for ODA, that is, development orientation of the loan and a minimum grant element of 25 percent based on a fixed 10 percent discount rate.

Paris Club creditors decide on a case-by-case basis whether a specific country receives nonconcessional or concessional terms largely on the basis of the income level of the debtor country. For the evolution of rescheduling terms see Table 5.2 on page 34.

Low-income countries that are classified by the World Bank as "IDA-only" (that is, can only borrow from the World Bank Group on concessional terms), and as PRGF-eligible by the IMF, are typically granted concessional rescheduling terms (cash-flow relief and NPV reduction) by Paris Club creditors.[47] Middle-income countries typically receive only cash-flow relief (nonconcessional terms) with shorter maturities. Rescheduling terms for both income groups have evolved over time with a lengthening of maturities, a move from flat to graduated repayment schedules,[48] and increased concessionality (in terms of present value reduction) for low-income countries. Middle-income countries historically received "standard terms" from the Paris Club until more favorable "Houston terms" were introduced in 1990 for lower middle-income countries. Standard terms for **upper-middle-income countries** were the following: for commercial (that is, non-ODA) debt, a flat repayment schedule applied with 9 years' maturity, including 5–6 years' grace, and market interest rates. ODA debt is rescheduled over 10 years with 5–6 years' grace at interest rates at least as concessional as the rates applying to the original credits. However, since the early 1990's, graduated repayment schedules have increasingly been applied with 2–3 years' grace and up to 15 years' maturity. This better reflects the projected recovery of the debtor's payment capacity, and yields earlier principal payments to creditors.

Houston terms for **lower middle-income countries** are more favorable with 15 years' maturity, including up to 8 years' grace, at market interest rates for commercial debt; and 20 years' maturity, including up to 10 years' grace for ODA debt at interest rates at least as concessional as the rates applying to the original credits. As is the case with standard terms, there has been an increasing use of graduated repayment schedules with up to 18 years' maturity, including up to 3 years' grace. On a voluntary basis, Houston terms also allow a limited amount of commercial debt to be converted in the framework of debt-for-nature, debt-for-aid, or other local currency debt swaps. Eligibility for Houston terms is guided by both income and debt burden criteria, based on World Bank data. In recent reschedulings, however, the distinction between standard terms and Houston terms has been blurred somewhat.

Rescheduling terms for **low-income countries** have become increasingly concessional over time. Since October 1988 they have included a reduction in the net present value of eligible debt: up to one-third under **Toronto terms**; this was increased to half under **London terms** since December 1991; and to two-thirds under **Naples terms** since January 1995. (Naples terms provide for both 50 percent NPV reduction and 67 percent reduction, decided on a case-by-case basis depending in principle on a country's income and indebtedness level.) Most reschedulings on Naples terms have been with a 67 percent NPV reduction. Figure A1 illustrates the evolution of payments profiles from Toronto to London, and Naples terms, clearly showing the lengthening of rescheduling terms and the reduction in the residual amounts payable.

[47]In some cases, however, low-income countries (for example, Kenya in 1994 and Ghana in 1996) have only requested a nonconcessional rescheduling of arrears in light of both the potential negative effect of Paris Club reschedulings on access to new financing, and of a limited financing need.

[48]Graduated payments (or "blended payments") refer, in the context of Paris Club reschedulings, to a repayment schedule where principal repayments (and therefore total repayments) gradually increase over the repayment period, reflecting an expected improvement in the repayment capacity of the country. Creditors have made increasing use of graduated payments, replacing flat payment schedules where equal amounts of principal repayments were made over the repayment period: from the creditor perspective, graduated payments provide for principal repayments starting earlier, and, from the debtor perspective, they avoid a large jump in debt service falling due.

Figure A1. Low-Income Rescheduling Profiles[1]
(Percent of amounts consolidated)

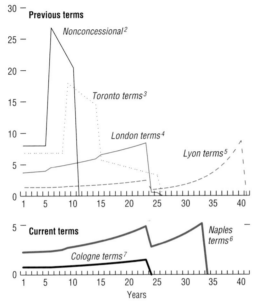

Sources: Paris Club Secretariat; and IMF staff estimates.

[1]Assuming a market interest rate of 8 percent. The payments profiles reflect the actual distribution of the debt reduction option (DR), debt service reduction option (DSR), the capitalization of moratorium interest option (CMI), or the long maturities option (LM). For an explanation of these terms, see the Glossary.

[2]Assuming equal principal repayments over 10 years including 5 years of grace.

[3]Equal distribution among the options (DR, DSR, and LM).

[4]Distribution (in percent) of DR 40; DSR 45; CMI 10; LM 5.

[5]80 percent reduction in NPV terms provided in the context of the original HIPC Initiative. Distribution (in percent) of DR 50; DSR 50.

[6]67 percent reduction in NPV terms. Distribution among options (in percent): DR 45; DSR 45; CMI 10. The LM option is not included, given that any creditor choosing this option undertakes best efforts to change to a concessional option at a later date when feasible.

[7]90 percent reduction in NPV terms provided in the context of the enhanced HIPC Initiative. DR option only.

In the context of the **HIPC Initiative**, creditors agreed in November 1996 to increase the NPV reduction up to 80 percent on eligible debt (Lyon terms) and in November 2000 to 90 percent (or more if needed; Cologne terms).[49] While the rescheduling terms, especially for low-income countries, have been standardized, creditors can choose from a menu of options to implement the debt relief. Among the options available to creditors to implement a concessional rescheduling, the most commonly used ones are the debt reduction option and the debt service reduction option. Under the **debt reduction option** (DR), creditors effect the required debt relief in net present value terms through a reduction of the principal of the consolidated amount; a commercial interest rate and standard repayment terms apply to the remaining amounts. Under the **debt service reduction option** (DSR), creditors effect the required debt relief in net present value terms through a reduction in the applicable interest rate. Under the **capitalization of moratorium interest option** (CMI), creditors effect the required NPV debt relief through a reduction in the applicable interest rate (but a lower reduction than in the debt service reduction option) and with a partial capitalization of moratorium interest. There is also a nonconcessional **long-maturities option** (LM) under which the consolidated amount is rescheduled over a long period of time, but without a reduction in the net present value of the debt; this is only used in the context of flow reschedulings as creditors have agreed to use concessional options only for stock-of-debt operation.

Some Paris Club creditors do not have legal authority to provide debt reduction on their claims so they always choose the DSR option. Some creditors switch options from agreement to agreement. Generally, creditors have the option also to provide a rescheduling in the form

---

[49]For further information on the HIPC Initiative, see Boote and Kamau (1999), and the IMF website: *www.imf.org.*

of new money, or to achieve a NPV reduction through the provision of grants.

Coverage and Subordination Strategy

Debt service that is *eligible* for rescheduling generally comprises all arrears and maturities falling due during an agreed period of time (the **consolidation period**) on medium- and long-term external government and government guaranteed debt or public sector debt contracted or disbursed before the **cutoff date**. The consolidation period typically coincides with the time span of the debtor's IMF arrangement.

Coverage under a Paris Club rescheduling, in other words, what debt service or arrears are rescheduled, depends on the financing need as shown in the IMF-supported program. Paris Club reschedulings have mostly been in the form of **flow reschedulings**, that is, rescheduling the flow of debt service payments falling due during, and arrears at the beginning of the consolidation period. Comprehensive coverage of a rescheduling agreement implies the inclusion of most or all eligible debt service and arrears. Reschedulings were often less comprehensive for countries expected to graduate from debt relief—coverage often declined over the course of a multiyear consolidation period. Only very few reschedulings for middle-income countries have included a treatment of the stock of debt, such as the agreements with Poland (1991) and Egypt (1994), and to a more limited extent, Russia and Peru (1996).[50] Most middle-income countries have already graduated from Paris Club reschedulings or are expected to graduate at the end of their current consolidation period.

In order to facilitate an exit from repeated reschedulings for low-income countries, creditors introduced the so-called "**stock-of-debt operations**" that treat the stock of eligible debt rather than a flow of debt service falling due over a limited period of time. London terms

provided for stock operations as early as 1991, but these have only been implemented since 1995 under Naples terms, and later on Lyon and Cologne terms.

Subordination Strategy

Official bilateral creditors have assisted countries with debt-servicing difficulties not only through debt rescheduling, but also through the provision of new financial assistance, often including new loans. With a view to minimizing the negative effects of reschedulings on new flows of financial assistance, Paris Club creditors set a **cutoff date** in a country's first rescheduling agreement: loans contracted after the cutoff date are protected and not expected to be subject to any future rescheduling. In other words, old debt (pre-cutoff date debt) is effectively subordinated to new debt (post-cutoff date debt). Until the mid-1980s cutoff dates were often moved later during subsequent reschedulings. With the advent of concessional reschedulings, however, the cutoff date has been maintained in virtually all rescheduling agreements since then.

Post-cutoff date debt. Paris Club creditors require that post-cutoff date debt be serviced on schedule. In very exceptional cases, where a large financing gap cannot be filled without treatment beyond eligible debt, creditors have been willing to defer on nonconcessional terms part of or all arrears (but not current maturities) on post-cutoff date debt. Such deferrals have been over a relatively short period of time, however, typically not longer than the end of the consolidation period.

Short-term debt. Paris Club creditors have also maintained a policy of not rescheduling short-term debt. In exceptional cases, however, creditors have agreed to defer arrears on short-term debt on nonconcessional terms when a clear need for such exceptional treatment was demonstrated in order to fill the financing gap of a program.

---

[50]These were flow reschedulings combined with some stock treatment of remaining debts at the end of the consolidation periods.

Pre-cutoff date debt. Paris Club creditors tailor the coverage of pre-cutoff date (medium- and long-term) debt in a rescheduling to the financing need in each case. They would usually cover debt not previously rescheduled (NPRD) and debt previously rescheduled on nonconcessional terms (PRD-NC). If necessary, they would consider to extend coverage to debt previously rescheduled on concessional terms—with a preference for treating obligations under older agreements rather than more recent ones. For concessional reschedulings under Naples terms, this includes the topping up of previous concessional terms (for example, Toronto- or London-terms debt) to the new, more favorable level of concessionality. Creditors have a strong preference not to include the payments resulting from the most recent past rescheduling agreement; the debtor should therefore make an effort to honor previous agreements. Only in cases of very large financing needs—on an exceptional basis—creditors may agree to include the last rescheduling agreement by deferring the debt concerned nonconcessionally.

Late interest. If the debtor country has been accumulating arrears, late interest has accrued on such arrears, and the amounts can be large if the arrears have been incurred over an extended period of time. Any inclusion of late interest under a Paris Club rescheduling depends largely on whether there is a financing need. Creditors determine the coverage of late interest arrears on a case-by-case basis.

Moratorium interest. This is interest due on the Paris Club rescheduling based on the terms of the Agreed Minute. In very exceptional cases of extremely limited payment capacity, creditors have agreed to defer part of the moratorium interest due.

De minimis creditors. Minor creditors are exempted from debt restructuring under the de minimis clause in order to simplify the implementation of a Paris Club rescheduling agreement. Their claims are payable in full as they fall due. An exposure limit defining a minor creditor is specified in each Agreed Minute, typically ranging from SDR 250,000 to SDR 1 million of consolidated debt.

Debt swaps. Paris Club Agreed Minutes for low-income and lower-middle-income countries usually include a clause that allows the conversion of commercial (non-ODA) debt on a voluntary basis in the context of debt-for-nature, debt-for-aid, debt-for-equity, or other local currency debt swaps. The limit on such transactions was raised in June 1996 to the greater of 20 percent of consolidated commercial credits outstanding, or SDR 15–30 million per creditor; the exact figure within this range is decided on a case-by-case basis. There are no limits on debt swaps of ODA loans.

Special accounts. In the context of the Paris Club, deposits into special accounts were first introduced in 1983 for debtor countries that had a history of accumulating external arrears. After signing the Agreed Minute, the debtor makes monthly deposits into an earmarked account at the central bank of one of the creditor countries. The deposit amounts are roughly equal to the moratorium interest that is expected to fall due on the rescheduled debt owed to all Paris Club creditors combined and any other payments falling due during the consolidation period. The debtor then draws on the deposited funds to make payments as soon as the bilateral agreements with the individual Paris Club creditors are signed and as other payments fall due. A debtor country needs to honor the monthly deposits required, but also remains responsible for effecting payments from the special account to creditors.

Implementation of Multiyear Rescheduling Agreements (MYRAs)

MYRAs are typically provided in support of multiyear IMF arrangements, and are implemented in two–three tranches, typically annual tranches. The first tranche of a MYRA usually becomes effective upon signature of the Agreed Minute, unless there is an entry-into-force clause that needs to be met first (normally a requirement that certain payments be made as of a specified date). The implementation of subsequent tranches normally requires that a debtor country remains current in its debt service to creditors, and the IMF Board has approved the second or third annual arrangement under an IMF-supported program as specified in the Agreed Minute. It requires explicit approval from the Paris Club, usually at a *tour d'horizon* discussion, and is communicated to the debtor country in writing by the Chairperson of the Paris Club.

Comparability of Treatment

A major objective of Paris Club creditors has been to assure equitable burden sharing of the costs associated with debt relief among creditors. The Paris Club attaches great importance to the principle that all creditors should bear their fair share of the burden of financial support for a debtor country; and that creditors not participating in reschedulings should not benefit unduly from relief offered by participating creditors. To avoid this "free rider" problem, all Paris Club agreements contain a clause under which the debtor country agrees to seek at least comparable terms to those obtained in the Paris Club rescheduling from other creditors, and not to grant other creditors a treatment more favorable than to Paris Club creditors. This general policy applies to all creditors to which the rescheduling country has significant debt service obligations—with the notable exception of multilateral institutions, whose preferred creditor status has long been implicitly accepted by Paris Club creditors (on the basis that multilaterals are providing net new money).

Comparable Treatment by Non-Paris Club Creditors

In assessing whether action taken by nonparticipating creditors is comparable to their own action, Paris Club creditors have not typically been concerned with the precise form that the debt restructuring takes, but rather with the effective relief provided in cash-flow and (to a lesser extent) in net present value terms. In keeping with the underlying concern that all creditors should participate in providing financial support for the debtor country, Paris Club creditors also take into account whether a nonparticipating creditor is providing new money. Judging comparability of treatment is more an art than a science, however, and ultimately it is up to Paris Club creditors themselves to assess whether a particular agreement with another bilateral or commercial creditor is "comparable" to the rescheduling terms granted by them. However, it should be pointed out that an agreement by debtor country authorities with a non-Paris Club creditor on terms that are clearly not comparable with those provided by the Paris Club is formally a breach of the debtor's Paris Club agreement that could lead Paris Club creditors to require the authorities to reopen the particular agreement with the creditor concerned, or, failing that, could lead to the termination of the Paris Club agreement. Such an action would in turn jeopardize the financing of the underlying IMF-supported program.

Bilateral Negotiations

The bilateral agreement. While the Agreed Minute of a Paris Club rescheduling sets out the general terms of the debt restructuring, the bilateral agreements concluded between the debtor country and each creditor country are the legal basis for implementing the restructuring and specify the debts concerned and the interest rate to be applied. Some creditor countries require not only a framework bilateral agreement, but also that the debtor country conclude individual agreements implementing the bilateral agreement with various national lending agencies involved in the rescheduling.

The bilateral deadline. Under the provisions contained in the Agreed Minute, the debtor country is expected to conclude the bilateral agreements with each creditor country without undue delay and, in any case, by the bilateral deadline. The period between the date of the

Agreed Minute and the bilateral deadline typically is some six–seven months.

Payments and effective cash-flow relief. No payments are due to creditors on rescheduled amounts until the bilateral agreement is signed—but payments on debt not consolidated or deferred, such as de minimis amounts or maturities falling due on post-cutoff date and short-term debt, are payable by the date specified "for all other payments" in the Agreed Minute or by their due date. Effectively, given the typical delays in signing bilateral agreements, the cash-flow relief of a rescheduling agreement is somewhat larger than implied by the Agreed Minute.

Determination of maturity and grace period. The Paris Club calculates the grace period and maturity from the middle of the consolidation period plus six months.

THE DEBT INITIATIVE FOR HEAVILY INDEBTED POOR COUNTRIES—KEY FEATURES AND PROGRESS

Since the debt crisis of the 1980s, the international financial community has been providing help to debtor countries in reducing their external debt burdens in order to foster growth, reduce poverty, and attain external viability. This assistance has taken the form of highly concessional financing from international financial institutions, debt relief from official creditors mainly in the context of Paris Club reschedulings and, in some cases, through bilateral action by official creditors. These measures have resulted in considerable success in alleviating the external debt burdens of many middle-income countries. Many poor countries, especially those in sub-Saharan Africa, however, have continued to suffer from unacceptable levels of poverty and heavy external debt burdens owing to a combination of factors, including poor governance, a lack of perseverance in structural adjustment and economic reform, and a deterioration in their terms of trade.

To address the problems of these countries, the World Bank and the IMF jointly launched in September 1996 the Initiative for the Heavily Indebted Poor Countries (HIPCs) to reduce the external debt burdens of all the eligible HIPCs to sustainable levels, provided they carry out strong programs of macroeconomic adjustment and structural reforms. In October 1999, the modalities of the Initiative were revised in light of the increased emphasis on poverty reduction in IMF- and Bank-supported programs. This Appendix gives a summary of the key features of the HIPC Initiative, the enhancements to the framework adopted in the fall of 1999 and progress in implementation thus far.[51]

The Key Features of the HIPC Initiative

The Initiative is intended to deal comprehensively with the overall external debt burden of eligible countries within a reasonable period of time. A country can be considered to achieve external debt sustainability if it is expected to be able to meet its current and future external debt service obligations in full, without recourse to debt relief, rescheduling of debts, or the accumulation of arrears, and without compromising economic growth. Debt relief under the HIPC Initiative is provided in two stages:

In the **first stage**, the debtor country needs to demonstrate the capacity to use prudently whatever debt relief is granted by adhering to IMF- and World Bank-supported structural adjustment programs. During this period, the country will receive debt relief from Paris Club creditors under traditional mechanisms (usually a flow rescheduling on Naples terms) and concessional financing from the multilateral institutions and bilateral donors.

At the beginning of the **second stage**, when the *decision point* under the Initiative is reached, the Executive Boards of the IMF and World Bank determine on the basis of the results of a debt sustainability analysis whether the full application of traditional debt relief mechanisms (Paris Club stock-of-debt operation on Naples terms involving a 67 percent NPV reduction with at least comparable action from non-Paris Club official bilateral and commercial creditors) would be sufficient for the country to reach sustainable levels of external debt, or whether additional assistance would be required under the Initiative. In the latter case, the IMF and the Bank would commit to granting debt relief, provided the country continues implementing macroeconomic reforms and structural adjustment policies, including strengthened social policies aimed at reducing poverty. At the same

---

[51]For a comprehensive description of the HIPC Initiative, see Andrews and others (1999).

time, Paris Club creditors provide additional debt relief through a flow rescheduling, and commit to providing at the end of the second stage, when the *completion point* has been reached, a stock-of-debt operation. The full amount of debt relief by the IMF and the World Bank will be provided at the completion point as well, on the condition that other creditors (including multilateral development banks, commercial creditors, and non-Paris Club official bilateral creditors) participate in the debt relief operation on comparable terms.

How the Enhanced HIPC Initiative Works

Following extensive consultations with interested parties from civil society and the Group of Seven meeting of heads of states in Cologne in June 1999, the Boards of the IMF and the World Bank agreed to a revision of the HIPC Initiative, to make debt relief broader, deeper, and faster, while strengthening the link between debt relief and poverty reduction. While the principle of providing debt relief in two stages and the crucial importance of implementing IMF- and Bank-supported adjustment programs has remained unchanged, the number of eligible countries has increased, the amount of debt relief each eligible country will receive has been raised, and its delivery accelerated. The modalities of the enhanced HIPC Initiative can be summarized as follows:

Targets of Debt Relief

- The external debt burden of a poor country is deemed sustainable, if the net present value of debt does not exceed 150 percent of exports or 250 percent of fiscal revenue. Under the original Initiative, the target for the NPV of debt-to-exports ratio was 200–250 percent, and for the debt-to-revenue ratio 280 percent.

- Eligibility for assistance under the fiscal window is subject to thresholds for the openness of an economy (export-to-GDP ratio) of 30 percent (was 40 percent under the original Initiative) and for the revenue effort (revenue-to-GDP ratio) of 15 percent (was 20 percent).[52]

Assessment Base

- The calculation of debt relief is based on actual debt data at the decision point; under the original Initiative, the committed debt relief was based on projections for the completion point. In most cases, this change in the calculation is likely to result in higher assistance since the debt ratios typically decline as economic reforms take hold. As a result of this change, there will no longer be a need for automatic reassessment at the completion point of the amount of assistance to be provided.

Delivery of Assistance

- The delivery of debt relief by the IMF and the World Bank under the enhanced HIPC framework starts in the form of interim assistance immediately after reaching the decision point, with the remainder of the debt reduction provided at the completion point.[53] Other multilateral institutions are expected to provide assistance on comparable terms. The provision of interim assistance under the enhanced Initiative is a major departure from the original framework, which provided for debt relief by international financial institutions only after reaching the completion point.

---

[52]The fiscal window under the Initiative has been established to ensure that heavily indebted poor countries with very open economies may have access to debt relief, even if they do not meet the minimum NPV of debt/export ratio. The identification of countries with exceptionally open economies is based on the exports/GDP ratio. The threshold for the revenue/GDP ratio aims to exclude those countries from debt relief under the fiscal window that exceed the targeted NPV of debt/revenue ratio because of serious shortcomings in their revenue mobilization efforts.

[53]In general, interim assistance provided by the IMF is subject to an upper limit of 60 percent of total assistance under the Initiative, and may not exceed the annual amount of debt service obligations due to the IMF.

- Paris Club creditors will provide assistance through a flow rescheduling on Cologne terms (with 90 percent NPV reduction), covering the period of the second stage followed by a stock-of-debt operation at the completion point to deliver the balance of the required debt relief. Under the original framework, Paris Club creditors provided debt relief on Lyon terms, with 80 percent NPV reduction.

- Other official bilateral and commercial creditors are expected to provide comparable debt relief.

Conditionality

- During the second stage, the country will need to make significant progress in stabilizing the economy, implementing structural reforms, and reducing poverty. The completion point will be reached when the country has met the agreed conditions for a floating completion point, which include the following:

  - The debtor country will need to continue to implement the financial and economic programs supported by the IMF's Poverty Reduction and Growth Facility and the World Bank aimed at achieving stable macroeconomic conditions.

  - To strengthen the link between debt relief and poverty reduction, the enhanced Initiative requires the preparation and implementation of a nationally owned, comprehensive poverty reduction strategy, as reflected in a Poverty Reduction Strategy Paper (PRSP).[54] A PRSP, prepared in broad consultation with civil society, should be in place and broadly endorsed by the Boards of the IMF and the Bank when a country reaches its decision point under the enhanced HIPC Initiative. During a transition period, a decision point may be agreed be-

fore the completion of a full PRSP on the basis of an *interim PRSP*, which summarizes the government's objectives of its poverty reduction strategy. This was the case for Bolivia, Mauritania, Tanzania, and Uganda, which reached their decision points under the enhanced framework in early 2000. In all cases, substantial progress in implementing the poverty reduction strategy is an important condition for reaching the completion point under the Initiative.

- Other creditors will need to confirm their participation in the debt relief operation.

Duration of the Second Stage

- Under the original framework, the length of the period between the decision and completion points (the second stage) was at least three years, assuming that the country would implement an IMF- and Bank-supported medium-term adjustment program according to schedule. The enhanced Initiative has adopted a more flexible approach with a *floating* completion point that will be reached when key structural reforms and certain major poverty reduction measures specified in the PRSP have been implemented, which could take less than three years.

Implementation

Thirty-six countries are expected to qualify for assistance under the enhanced HIPC Initiative, most of which are in sub-Saharan Africa. As of end-December 2000, 22 countries had reached their decision points under the enhanced framework (Benin, Bolivia, Burkina Faso, Cameroon, Gambia, Guinea, Guinea-Bissau, Guyana, Honduras, Madagascar, Malawi, Mali, Mauritania, Mozambique, Nicaragua, Niger, Rwanda, São Tomé and Príncipe, Senegal, Tanzania, Uganda, and Zambia), and Uganda had also reached its completion point (Table A1). Total committed

---

[54]The strategy should include measures to improve the delivery of social services, improve expenditure controls and budget management, and strengthen external debt management.

Table A1. HIPC Initiative: Status of Country Cases Considered Under the Initiative, January 31, 2001

Country	Decision Point	Completion Point	Target NPV of Debt-to- Exports (Percent)	Target NPV of Debt-to- Government revenue (Percent)	Total	Assistance Levels[1] (Millions of U.S. dollars, present value) Bilateral	Multilateral	IMF	World Bank	Percentage Reduction in NPV of Debt[2]	Estimated Total Nominal Debt Service Relief (Millions of U.S. dollars)
Completion point reached under enhanced framework											
Uganda					1,003	183	820	160	517		1,950
original framework	Apr. 97	Apr. 98	202		347	73	274	69	160	20	650
enhanced framework	Feb. 00	May 00	150		656	110	546	91	357	37	1,300
Decision point reached under enhanced framework											
Benin	Jul. 00	Floating	150		265	77	189	24	84	31	460
Bolivia					1,302	425	876	84	194		2,060
original framework	Sep. 97	Sep. 98	225		448	157	291	29	53	14	760
enhanced framework	Feb. 00	Floating	150		854	268	585	55	141	30	1,300
Burkina Faso					398	56	342	42	162		700
original framework	Sep. 97	Jul. 00	205		229	32	196	22	91	27	400
enhanced framework	Jul. 00	Floating	150		169	24	146	20	71	27	300
Cameroon	Oct. 00	Floating	150		1,260	874	324	37	179	27	2,000
Gambia, The	Dec. 00	Floating	150		67	17	49	2	22	27	90
Guinea	Dec. 00	Floating	150		545	215	328	31	152	32	800
Guinea-Bissau	Dec. 00	Floating	150		416	212	204	12	93	85	790
Guyana					585	220	365	74	68		1,030
original framework	Dec. 97	May 99	107	280	256	91	165	35	27	24	440
enhanced framework	Nov. 00	Floating	150	250	329	129	200	40	41	40	590
Honduras	Jun. 00	Floating	110	250	556	215	340	30	98	18	900
Madagascar	Dec. 00	Floating	150		814	457	357	22	252	40	1,500
Malawi	Dec. 00	Floating	150		643	163	480	30	331	44	1,000
Mali					523	162	361	58	182		870
original framework	Sep. 98	Sep. 00	200		121	37	84	14	44	9	220
enhanced framework	Sep. 00	Floating	150		401	124	277	44	138	28	650
Mauritania	Feb. 00	Floating	137	250	622	261	361	47	100	50	1,100
Mozambique					1,970	1,235	736	140	434		4,300
original framework	Apr. 98	Jun. 99	200		1,716	1,076	641	125	381	63	3,700
enhanced framework	Apr. 00	Floating	150		254	159	95	16	53	9	600
Nicaragua	Dec. 00	Floating	150		3,267	2,145	1,123	82	189	72	4,500
Niger	Dec. 00	Floating	150		521	211	309	28	170	54	890
Rwanda	Dec. 00	Floating	150		452	56	397	44	228	71	814

São Tomé and Príncipe	Dec. 00	Floating	150		97	29	68	—	24	83	200
Senegal	Jun. 00	Floating	133		488	193	259	45	124	19	850
Tanzania	Apr. 00	Floating	150		2,026	1,006	1,020	120	695	54	3,000
Zambia	Dec. 00	Floating	150	250	2,499	1,168	1,331	602	493	63	3,820
Decision point reached under original framework											
Côte d'Ivoire	Mar. 98	Mar. 01	141	280	345	163	182	23	91	6 [3]	800
Total assistance provided/committed					20,663	9,744	1,082[1]	1,737[4]	4,883		34,424
Preliminary HIPC document issued[5]											
Chad	...	...	150		157	34	123	15	65	27	250
Ethiopia	...	...	200		636	225	411	22	214	23	1,300

Sources: IMF and World Bank Board decisions, completion point documents, decision point documents, preliminary HIPC documents, and staff calculations.

[1] Assistance levels are at countries' respective decision or completion points, as applicable.

[2] In percent of the net present value of debt at the decision or completion point (as applicable), after the full use of traditional debt-relief mechanisms.

[3] Nonreschedulable debt to non-Paris Club official bilateral creditors and the London Club, which was already subject to a highly concessional restructuring, is excluded from the NPV of debt at the completion point in the calculation of this ratio.

[4] Equivalent to SDR 1,338 million at an SDR/USD exchange rate of 0.7705.

[5] Figures are based on preliminary assessments at the time of the issuance of the preliminary HIPC document; and are subject to change. Assistance level for Ethiopia is based on the original framework and applied at the completion point; for Chad, targets are based on the enhanced framework and assistance levels are at the assumed decision point.

assistance to these 22 countries is $34 billion in future debt service savings, or $21 billion in NPV terms, representing an average debt reduction in net present value terms of more than 45 percent on top of traditional debt relief mechanisms. In addition, Côte d'Ivoire had reached its decision point under the original framework. Total assistance under the HIPC Initiative committed to Côte d'Ivoire amounted to $345 million, and will be reassessed under the enhanced Initiative.

For more information on the HIPC Initiative, see the IMF website, where all related documents are posted at *www.imf.org/hipc*.

DEBT RELIEF UNDER "TRADITIONAL MECHANISMS"

The arrival of the millennium and the associated campaign to cancel the debt of low-income countries has heightened public awareness of initiatives to solve the debt crisis of low-income countries (LICs). The history of debt relief efforts for low-income countries goes back at least two decades.

During the 1970s and early 1980s many developing countries experienced a sharp increase in their external borrowing. Middle-income countries were mainly borrowing from private creditors, especially commercial banks. Most low-income countries, however, had more restricted access to private finance and were more often contracting loans either directly from other governments or their export credit agencies (ECAs) or through private loans, which had been insured for payment by an ECA.

While private creditors typically reduced their exposure and cut their losses in response to the LIC payments difficulties of the early and mid-1980s, the immediate response of official creditors came in the form of comprehensive nonconcessional rescheduling, known as "flow reschedulings" in the context of the Paris Club. This was combined with new lending from multilateral agencies such as the IMF and the multilateral development banks, as well as some additional credits from the ECAs. The then Soviet Union also continued to provide substantial financing to countries with which it had close ties. In responding to the payments crisis, therefore, the official creditors were willing to take risks well beyond those acceptable to private commercial lenders in order to support the adjustment programs of the debtor countries concerned.

Flow reschedulings in the Paris Club involved the creditors accepting to delay receipt of payments falling due during the period of an economic program supported by the IMF, and to reschedule such amounts for eventual repayment over the medium and long term. As the 1980s progressed, LIC Paris Club reschedulings increasingly involved the delay of most or all principal and interest payments falling due. From 1976 to 1988 the Paris Club agreed 81 nonconcessional flow reschedulings with 27 of the countries now identified as HIPCs (Table A2). These nonconcessional flow reschedulings allowed for payments equivalent to about $23 billion to be delayed into the future. The average debt service paid by HIPCs nonetheless increased from about 17 percent of exports in 1980 to a peak of about 30 percent of exports in 1986.[55] While this approach provided substantial cash flow relief, and allowed comprehensive adjustment programs to be fully financed, the frequent rescheduling of debt service payments (especially the capitalization of interest) also contributed to a steady increase in the debt stocks outstanding.

From Toronto Terms to Naples Terms

The acceptance by the Paris Club in 1987 of a proposal by the U.K. Chancellor of the Exchequer to reschedule LICs' debt at below market rates of interest marked a watershed in the financing of low-income countries. Thus, for the first time it was proposed that reschedulings of commercially priced ECA debt should involve a reduction in the present value of the debt outstanding. Governments were now being asked to formally acknowledge and finance past losses on their ECA activities. In addition, about one year after the introduction of the concessional Structural Adjustment Facility, the Managing

[55]The analysis and cost estimates presented in this appendix are based on Daseking and Powell (1999). See also Stephens (1999).

Table A2. HIPCs: Paris Club Reschedulings by Type of Terms, 1976–2000

	Number of Countries	Amount Consolidated (Millions of U.S. dollars)	Number of Reschedulings	Stock or Flow
Toronto terms	19	5,984	27	flow deals only
London terms	22	8,774	24	flow deals only
Naples terms	28	16,325	35	7 stock deals
Lyon terms	5	4,875	6	4 stock deals
Cologne terms	7	984	7	1 stock deal
Nonconcessional	29	23,738	89	flow deals only

Sources: Paris Club Secretariat, and IMF staff estimates.

Director of the IMF, put forward a plan for an enhanced concessional IMF lending window for LICs—the Enhanced Structural Adjustment Facility (ESAF). This, too, would be financed by grants from the wealthier countries. Both these initiatives had as their goal a desire to avoid the debts of LICs rising in an unsustainable way, and to limit any significant new nonconcessional lending or refinancing to poor countries. Under the flow rescheduling approach, creditors were able to agree to receive no payments at all during the consolidation period except interest on the rescheduled amounts (moratorium interest); in exceptional circumstances creditors even agreed to defer this as well. Even so, to the extent the rescheduling terms were nonconcessional, this implied no reduction in the present value of debts being rescheduled, and hence no accounting loss. The perceived problem was therefore not cash flow, but an excessive and unsustainable buildup of the stock of debt—a "debt overhang."

While the U.K. proposals were to lower the interest rates charged on reschedulings, the French suggested reducing payments falling due by a third, while rescheduling the remainder at appropriate market interest rates. The U.S., however, was at that time unable to accept any form of present value reduction (accounting loss) but accepted to reschedule with longer grace periods—although this would not affect the book value of their claims, which continued to be valued at 100 cents on the dollar. Eventually a compromise was reached at the Toronto G-7 summit in 1988, providing Paris Club creditors with a menu of these three options, loosely considered to be comparable. These became known as the *Toronto terms*.

From 1988–91, 20 LICs received reschedulings on Toronto terms, with about $6 billion of payments falling due being either partially cancelled or rescheduled on a concessional basis. As early as 1990, however, it was clear to many Paris Club creditors that the concessions—or present value debt reductions—provided under Toronto terms would be insufficient to prevent the continued and unsustainable rise in the debt stocks. While the Paris Club had the tools available to continue to provide immediate cash flow assistance to LICs, medium-term repayment profiles associated with the rescheduling agreements were increasingly seen as unrealistic (see Figure A1 and Table A3). In September 1990, John Major, as U.K. Chancellor of the Exchequer, argued at the Commonwealth Finance Minister's meeting in Trinidad that a present value reduction of two-thirds (67 percent) would be more realistic for LICs, and that the full stock of a country's eligible debt needed to be addressed in a single operation.

Paris Club creditors instead agreed to increase the degree of concessionality to 50 percent in 1991, under what became known as the *London terms*. Creditors did, however, accept that after a period of good performance—typically 3 years—they would be willing to discuss the possibility of an agreement covering the full stock of debt. It was not until the Naples G-7 economic summit in 1994, that a consensus emerged to deepen the concessions to 67 percent; *Naples terms* were implemented from January 1995. In the period

Table A3. HIPC Debt Stocks Before and After Assistance

(Billions of U.S. dollars)

	32 Countries Expected to Receive Assistance (excl. Sudan, Somalia, Liberia)
Nominal debt end-1997 (GDF)[1]	126
NPV of debt end-1997 (GDF)[1, 2]	98
NPV of debt after traditional mechanism	66
Less NPV of HIPC assistance	29
NPV of debt after HIPC assistance	37

Sources: *Global Development Finance* (GDF), 1999; and IMF staff estimates.

[1]GDF values Russian ruble debt at the official exchange rate of R0.6/$.

[2]GDF methodology for calculating present value does not correspond exactly to that used in the HIPC Initiative, which uses detailed loan-by-loan data and currency-specific discount rates.

1991–mid-1999, 26 rescheduling agreements were signed under London terms, and a further 34 under Naples terms—seven of which covered the full stock of eligible debt—with a total of about $25 billion of payments being either partially forgiven or rescheduled at low interest rates over the medium and long term.

The slow progress in reducing official debt stocks largely reflected accounting and budgetary concerns and the need for a consensus to develop among all the major creditor agencies involved. Creditors saw their relations with LICs in different ways, and this was reflected in their approach to establish the appropriate combination of debt relief, new lending, and grant financing—as well as in their assessment of the importance of conditionality. While debt stocks were clearly rising well beyond sustainable levels in many cases, Paris Club creditors were able to use concessional rescheduling techniques to contain the growth of payments actually being requested. In practice, the average paid debt service ratios for HIPCs, after peaking at about 26 percent of exports in 1986, fell fairly steadily to about 15 percent by 1999 (Figure A2, lower

panel). Rescheduling helped to ensure that after other official support was taken into account, overall official transfers to LICs remained highly positive throughout the period. Reflecting the adoption of more concessional rescheduling terms and the impact of stock-of-debt operations, as well as more concessional new financing, the present value of debt-to-exports ratios began to fall after 1992.

Estimates of Debt Relief

Concessional reschedulings, culminating in Paris Club stock-of-debt operations on Naples terms, together with debt relief by non-Paris Club official bilateral and commercial creditors on at least comparable terms,[56] have conventionally become known as *traditional debt relief mechanisms,* a term used in the context of the HIPC Initiative. Traditional mechanisms are defined here as all measures of debt relief that are not provided in the context of the HIPC Initiative. This includes specifically concessional flow reschedulings, stock-of-debt operations, and bilateral forgiveness of ODA claims by Paris Club creditors; reschedulings and bilateral debt forgiveness by non-Paris Club official bilateral creditors; and private commercial debt relief and buy-back operations.

The debt relief generated by these operations can be measured in two principal ways: (i) as cash-flow relief, which is generated whenever debt service payments falling due are canceled, rescheduled, or temporarily deferred; and (ii) as a reduction in the present value of the debt outstanding. The distinction between these two definitions is important and should not be confused. The cash-flow relief produced by a flow rescheduling operation is important for countries facing immediate severe balance of payments or fiscal financing constraints, but the relief is limited to the consolidation period and it adds to future debt service obligations even if it is accompanied by a reduction in the net

---

[56]The provision to seek at least comparable terms on non-Paris Club official bilateral and commercial debt is required of the debtor country, whenever it signs an agreement with the Paris Club.

Figure A2: Debt Burden Ratios, 1980–99
(Percent of exports of goods and services)

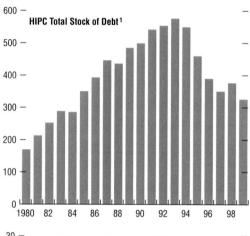

HIPC Total Stock of Debt[1]

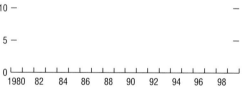

Total Debt Service Paid by Low-, Middle-Income,
and Heavily Indebted Poor Countries[2]

Source: World Bank, *Global Development Finance*, 2001.
[1]Aggregate stock of debt as a percent of aggregate exports.
[2]Aggregate debt service as a percent of aggregate exports.

present value of debt. The NPV reduction measures the discounted stream of all future debt service payments, which are forgiven as a result of the operation, and thus captures the concessional element involved. It thereby allows a meaningful comparison of the effective relief provided across the various rescheduling methods chosen by different creditors. Estimates of debt relief reported below focus on the NPV effects of the various debt relief mechanisms, and are directly comparable to the methods used for costing the HIPC Initiative.

The Paris Club is estimated to have provided about **$23 billion** of NPV relief under its concessional rescheduling terms since 1988 (excluding Russia and non-Paris Club bilaterals, and Paris Club forgiveness of ODA debt). The IDA debt reduction facility accounts for a further $5 billion of NPV relief. These figures are, therefore, probably lower bounds on the amount of actual debt relief that has been provided in the period since 1988. If debt relief by Russia for low-income countries is valued after the up-front discount agreed with Paris Club creditors, then this would add about $8 billion—raising the total NPV debt relief to about **$36 billion**.[57]

The debt initiatives prior to the HIPC Initiative have, therefore, had a significant effect on the debt burden of LICs. The enhanced HIPC Initiative is expected to bring debt burden ratios down even further to levels last seen in the 1970s. While different definitions can yield different average debt service ratios, it is clear that the various initiatives from 1988 onwards have helped lower debt service payments of HIPCs from about 26 percent of exports in the mid-1980s to about 15 percent by 1999, and below the aggregate level for LICs more generally. The HIPC Initiative was designed to build on and reinforce these past efforts. Total assistance (beyond traditional mechanisms) expected to be provided through the HIPC

[57]If the up-front discount on Russian claims, valued at the official exchange rate, is included, this total would increase to about $60 billion.

Initiative is currently estimated at about **$29 billion**, in 1999 present value terms.[58]

At end-1999, the present value of debt of the 32 HIPCs included in these cost estimates was about $93 billion. Estimates prepared in the context of the HIPC Initiative costing exercise suggest that the present value of the external debt of these countries after the hypothetical full application of all traditional debt relief mechanisms would be about $69 billion. After HIPC assistance, the stock of debts is estimated to fall to about $40 billion in present value terms.

[58]The $29 billion figure excludes potential costs for Sudan, Somalia, or Liberia. Including these countries the estimated cost of the enhanced HIPC Initiative is about $37 billion, in 1999 present value terms, although the estimates for these countries are particularly weak.

THE IMF'S POVERTY REDUCTION AND GROWTH FACILITY (PRGF)

In September 1999, the objectives of the IMF's concessional lending were broadened to include an explicit focus on poverty reduction in the context of a growth-oriented strategy. The IMF will support, along with the World Bank, strategies elaborated by the borrowing country in a Poverty Reduction Strategy Paper (PRSP), which will be prepared with the participation of civil society—including the poor—and other development partners. Reflecting the new objectives and procedures, the IMF established the Poverty Reduction and Growth Facility (PRGF) to replace the Enhanced Structural Adjustment Facility (ESAF).

The ESAF concessional lending facility was set up in 1987 to help the IMF's poorest members in their efforts to achieve satisfactory economic growth and a sustained improvement in their balance of payments.

Much was achieved over the decade that followed. Growth rates of real per capita income in countries supported by the ESAF rose sharply in the second half of the 1990s—to rates almost double those of other developing countries. Key social indicators also improved, in part because ESAF-supported programs provided for increases in health and education spending averaging 4 percent a year in real per capita terms.

But it became increasingly apparent that more needed to be done to achieve faster growth and broader-based poverty reduction. While the underlying objective of IMF-supported policies has always been the attainment of sustainable growth, there was a growing realization of the need for policies aimed directly at assisting the poor, allowing them to benefit from, and contribute to, growth by expanding their economic opportunities. At the same time, investing in health, education, rural infrastructure, and private sector development—to name a few priorities—could be particularly effective in boosting growth.

From this, and growing out of the analysis and recommendations made in the internal and external reviews of the ESAF, and from the constructive suggestions of many outside commentators, came a commitment to making IMF-supported programs for low-income countries better integrated with policies to fight poverty, and with stronger and broader national ownership.

As a result, the September 1999 Interim and Development Committee Meetings endorsed the creation of a new facility, the Poverty Reduction and Growth Facility, to replace the ESAF. The PRGF functions alongside the debt relief program—the Heavily Indebted Poor Countries Initiative (HIPC)—of the IMF and the World Bank.

Poverty Reduction Strategies

Nationally-owned poverty reduction strategies are at the heart of the new approach. Programs supported by the PRGF (and the World Bank's concessional window—IDA) are being framed around a comprehensive, nationally owned Poverty Reduction Strategy Paper prepared by the borrowing country and endorsed in their respective areas of responsibility by the Executive Boards of the IMF and World Bank as the basis for the institutions' concessional loans and for relief under the enhanced HIPC Initiative.

Hence, the country and its people take the lead. PRSPs are prepared by the government, based on a process involving the active participation of civil society, NGOs, donors, and international institutions. It is expected that governments will keep civil society informed about developments in the program, and involved in monitoring its implementation. Locally produced PRSPs are expected to generate fresh ideas about strategies and measures needed to reach shared growth and poverty reduction goals, and to help develop a sense of ownership and national commitment to reaching those objectives.

The IMF and World Bank assist in the process, and other multilateral and bilateral donors are also providing advice and expertise. But the strategy and the policies should emerge out of national debates in which the voices of the poor, especially, are heard.

New PRGF-Supported Programs

The transformation of ESAF into the Poverty Reduction and Growth Facility has important implications for the design of programs supported by the IMF in low-income countries. The emphasis on growth and poverty reduction should directly influence policy choices, as well as the pace and sequencing of policy implementation. The concrete changes expected include the following:

- Budgets that are more pro-poor and pro-growth. IMF and World Bank advice to countries will emphasize further reorientation of government spending toward the social sectors, basic infrastructure, or other activities that help the poor to participate more fully in, and benefit more from, their country's achievement of economic growth. Improvements in the efficiency and targeting of public expenditure will be highlighted, as will opportunities for tax reforms that can simultaneously improve efficiency and equity.

- Greater flexibility in fiscal targets. The IMF will more actively seek additional financial assistance for countries that need more money to implement well-designed and well-executed poverty reduction strategies. The assistance must be provided on highly concessional terms so as not to add to countries' debt burdens. Limits on budget deficits under PRGF-supported programs will accommodate these extra resources.

- More emphasis on improving public resource management. Carefully designed and targeted antipoverty programs will not work unless the countries' governments have systems in place to ensure that money is not misspent. The development of effective mechanisms to monitor and control government spending at all levels, and with greater public accountability, is therefore expected to feature prominently in PRGF-supported programs.

- Protecting the poor during adjustment and reform. Promoting growth and long-term poverty reduction sometimes requires macroeconomic adjustments or structural reforms that can have a negative impact on some groups of poor people in the short run. Programs need to address the likely social impacts of reform programs and include measures to mitigate any adverse ones. The IMF and World Bank staffs will help governments identify situations where such measures are needed and incorporate them into countries' programs.

- More selective conditionality. ESAF-supported programs have typically made loan disbursements conditional on a wide array of structural reforms. Conditionality under the PRGF will focus more specifically on those monetary, fiscal, and institutional measures identified in the country's PRSP as being central to the maintenance of macroeconomic stability and growth and the effective management of public resources.

Implementation

Implementation of the new approach is well under way. The work of converting ESAF-supported programs that were in place in late 1999 to the PRGF began immediately. The number of new, three-year country programs conceived from the start as PRGF-supported arrangements is rapidly increasing. All poverty reduction strategies underpinning these programs are being published, as are most of the countries' program documents, and interested readers are encouraged to seek the latest information on the IMF's website at *www.imf.org*.

INTERNATIONAL SOCIAL DEVELOPMENT GOALS AND PERFORMANCE INDICATORS

Since the early 1990s, various global UN conferences have established goals for social policies, as well as for the environment, human settlements, human rights, drug control, and crime prevention. In particular, the Copenhagen Declaration on Social Development (March 1995) laid out a program of action for social development, which included the goals of eradicating poverty, promoting social integration, and achieving universal and equitable access to education and primary health care.

Key goals of social development are, by the year 2015, to:

- reduce the proportion of people living in poverty by at least one-half relative to 1993;

- achieve universal primary education in all countries;

- make progress toward gender equality by eliminating gender disparity in primary and secondary education (to be achieved by 2005);

- reduce maternal mortality rates by three-fourths and reduce infant and child mortality rates by two-thirds relative to 1990; and

- provide access to reproductive health services to all individuals of appropriate ages.

Indicators for Measuring Progress

Since the Copenhagen Declaration, several sets of social indicators have been identified in various forums to assess social development and monitor key social development goals. Examples of such sets of indicators are as follows:

- the OECD/UN/World Bank core set of working indicators of international development goals;[59]

- the Common Country Assessment (CCA) indicators of the UN Development Assistance Framework (UNDAF);

- the indicators of UN/CCA Task Force on Basic Social Services for All (BSSA); and

- the UN Statistical Commission's Minimum National Social Data Set (MNSDS).[60]

The OECD, World Bank, and UN, in cooperation with developing countries and bilateral donors, have established the following working set of **core indicators on social development**:

- *Poverty:* share of population living below $1 a day in purchasing power parity terms; the poverty gap (the resources needed to lift all those below the poverty line out of poverty); prevalence of underweight children under 5 years of age; and the share of the poorest 20 percent in national consumption;

- *Education:* net enrollment rates in primary education; completion rate of 4th grade of primary education; and literacy rate of those between 15 and 24 years of age;

- *Gender equality:* ratio of girls to boys in primary and secondary education; ratio of literate females to males (ages 15 to 24);

- *Health:* infant mortality rate; under-five mortality rate; maternal mortality rate; percentage of births attended by skilled personnel; contraceptive prevalence rate; and HIV prevalence in pregnant women ages 15 to 24 (for lack of data, currently the overall HIV prevalence rate is used).

---

[59]Available on the website: *http://www.oecd.org/dac/indicators/htm/tables.htm.*

[60]These indicators and their definitions are available in the World Bank's World Development Indicators database, and in the UNDP *Human Development Reports,* available on *http://www.undp.org/hdro/indicators.html#developing.*

In addition, the OECD/UN/World Bank core list includes six environment indicators, as well as ten background indicators of development, such as adult literacy rate, total fertility rate, and life expectancy.

The CCA/UNDAF list includes all indicators in the OECD/UN/World Bank core set, but for some development goals, the list has a more extensive scope, including, for example, more indicators on gender equality and women's empowerment, child welfare, and food security. In addition, the CCA/UNDAF list has indicators relating to employment, housing, drug control, and crime prevention.

Compared with the CCA/BSSA and MNSDS sets, the OECD/UN/World Bank list is more extensive and includes a wider range of social development indicators. However, the CCA/ BSSA and MNSDS sets also include some indicators not found in the OECD/UN/World Bank list, such as average years of schooling (MNSDS) and access to primary health care services (BSSA).

DEBT SWAPS AND THE PARIS CLUB

The market for debt swaps has been developed mainly in the context of market-based debt reduction schemes that made use of the existence of a secondary market in developing country debt, especially debt to commercial banks. These schemes emerged as part of the mechanism to deal with the debt crises of the early 1980s, and were utilized by Argentina, Brazil, Chile, Mexico, Peru, and the Philippines, among other countries. Swaps involving official bilateral creditors have been undertaken by a number of creditors mostly in the 1990s. Paris Club creditors swapped claims of $4.5 billion during the period 1991– April 2000, about 40 percent of which involved claims on Egypt.[61]

Types of Swaps

A swap arrangement transforms one type of asset into another with different characteristics and/or currency denomination. The most common swap arrangements are: debt-for-equity swap, debt-for-aid or development swap, debt-for-nature swap, debt-for-local-currency swap (also known as debt-for-peso swap), and debt-for-debt swap (see Box A1).

Benefits

Data provided by Paris Club creditors indicate that during 1991–April 2000, debt-for-equity swaps were the most important category of debt swaps involving official creditors. There are no comparable data on private sector debt swaps, but it seems reasonable to assume that debt-for-equity swaps are even more important in the private sector.

A creditor may decide to participate in debt-for-equity swaps for a variety of reasons. By selling a loan, a creditor may aim at improving the return on its assets, reducing exposure on the debtor country, or overcoming liquidity constraints. Also, the creditor may improve its capital/asset ratio, as the amount of loan loss reserves set aside may be greater than the discount on the asset. In case of undertaking the investment directly, bypassing the secondary market, a creditor can perhaps preserve the book value of its assets. Debt-for-equity swaps also allow creditors—especially commercial banks and multinational firms—to enter into accelerated remittances deals, in which a large share of the remittable cash flow is given to the creditor by the partner firm in exchange for a gradual redemption of the creditor's equity stake. In this way, the creditor can gradually reduce its stake in the investment to the benefit of a partner with a long-term investment objective.

The principal benefit to a debtor country from a debt-for-equity swap is a reduction in its debt-service burden. By converting a debt obligation into direct or portfolio investments, the debtor country's external debt is reduced, which might benefit the country's economic growth by reducing the debt overhang, as the debt overhang limits investment. Debt-for-equity swaps can help a privatization process and can contribute to the development of local capital markets and stock exchanges. Similarly, reinvestment of part of the dividend flows can provide a source of investable funds. In the case of new assets created by a debt-for-local-currency swap, debt service would be required only in local currency. In the case of countries where creditors, especially commercial banks, are reluctant to lend new resources, they may be more interested in reducing their credit exposure by converting their sovereign debt into

[61]This is based on a compilation by the Paris Club of data through April 2000.

Box A1. Types of Debt Swaps

The main players in a **debt-for-equity swap** arrangement are a creditor (commercial bank), an investor, and an indebted country. The basic mechanism for implementing a debt-equity swap involves the following steps. First, the creditor offers to sell at a discount an outstanding sovereign or government-guaranteed debt. Second, an investor, mostly a multinational company (or an individual or domestic investor), buys the debt at a discount and submits it to the central bank of the indebted country, which redeems the debt at the face value of the loan—or at a discount if the transaction involves debt forgiveness—in domestic currency at the official exchange rate. Third, with the domestic currency proceeds, the investor buys equity in an authorized industry or firm.

A **host debtor** country wishing to establish a swap program would need to decide whether to institute a transaction-by-transaction approval mechanism or a more general one based on broader categories of debt or creditors; to stipulate the debt instruments eligible for conversion and the amounts of local currency to be exchanged for the debt; to establish the priority investment areas and the corresponding discounts for incentive purposes at which the debt will be redeemed; to introduce dividend and capital repatriation regulations specifying timing and amounts of conformity with existing foreign investment taxes.

A (commercial bank) **creditor** engaging in swap arrangements would need to take into consideration home country regulations regarding swaps and ownership of foreign assets; host country regulations regarding debt swaps; tax treatment of debt-swap transactions (does the sale of a debt obligation at a discount qualify for a tax deduction); portfolio contamination (selling a specific loan at a discount and recording a loss may require adjusting downwards (mark-to-market) values of similar loans); and whether converted debt will be excluded from future new money packages a creditor (bank) may be required to commit as part of some future reschedulings.

An **investor** acquiring equity through debt swaps would have to consider the conditions re-garding capital repatriation and profit remittances on investments financed by debt conversion and those on regular direct investment; tax treatment of the gain from the difference between the purchase price and the redemption price; whether the original creditor, the debt itself, and the original borrower are eligible to participate in the official debt-swap scheme.

Debt-for-aid or development swap typically involves a creditor country converting its credits to a debtor country into local currency (mostly at a discount) with the agreement that the debtor country would spend the local currency equivalent on a development project previously agreed upon. Such swaps can, and increasingly do, involve a (foreign) nongovernmental organization (NGO), which may purchase the debt from the original creditor country at a discount using its own foreign exchange resources and then re-selling it to the debtor country with the agreement that the local currency proceeds would be spent on a development project. Another variation of this type of swap is transferring the local currency equivalent to a nongovernmental organization in the debtor country.

Debt-for-nature swaps are similar to debt-for-development swaps except that the funds are used for projects that improve and protect the environment in the debtor country. In some cases such an agreement may be made by a creditor country that is being adversely affected by pollution caused by environmentally damaging activities in the debtor country.

In the case of **debt-for-local-currency swaps**, residents instead of a foreign investor buy their own country's debt in the secondary market using funds they hold abroad or foreign currency acquired in the exchange market. They present the claims to the central bank or the original borrower for redemption. Assets are re-denominated in the local currency, as in a debt-equity swap, but the proceeds may not have to be invested directly to acquire equity in a local firm. In principle, the new assets created by such a swap would require future servicing only in local currency. These swaps are designed primarily for the repatriation of flight capital.

Box A1 *(concluded)*

Debt-for-debt swaps involve a change of creditors without otherwise changing the terms of repayment of their respective loans. The swap may be between external creditors (for example, a U.S. bank swapping Argentine debt with a European bank for Chilean debt), or it may involve a domestic creditor (for example, a Brazilian bank swapping its holdings of Mexican debt for Brazilian debt with a U.S. bank). These swaps do not result in debt conversion directly; however, they can be used to accumulate debt for conversion into equity, or merely allow banks to consolidate their exposures in a country where they have a long-term strategic interest.

shares of private companies with prospects of higher financial returns. A debt-for-equity swap program sends a positive signal to investors that a country is welcoming investment. Discounts inherent in a debt-for-equity swap may advance the timing of foreign investment as investment planned for the future may be brought forward to take advantage of what may be perceived as temporarily favorable terms of purchasing domestic assets.

Finally, for the third party investor, the main benefit is acquiring investment capital on more favorable terms—reflecting the discount involved—than those available through direct exchange market purchases of domestic currency.

Downsides

Debt swap operations may also have downsides, including distortions resulting from the subsidy elements of the operation; a lack of transparency; possible adverse monetary and fiscal effects; and the possibility of "round-tripping." These problems mainly relate to debt-for-equity swaps.

As noted above, debt-for-equity swaps may allow investors to reduce the total acquisition cost of the investment because of the discount on the debt instruments that are swapped. In the case of debt instruments traded in the secondary market (such as bonds), this discount represents market perceptions of the debtor country's ability to meet its future debt service obligations. As the debtor country could have benefitted from the discount by buying back the bonds in the open market or launching a favorable exchange offer, the discount effectively represents an investment subsidy from the debtor country to the investor. In the case of debt-for-equity swaps involving official debt, the discount is usually offered by the creditor country, which effectively constitutes a subsidy of the creditor country to the investor. In addition, debt-for-equity swaps often include other elements of subsidy, such as preferential tax treatment or below-market exchange rates for the conversion of the debt instruments in the local currency that is used to purchase the assets. As a result, the debtor country may attract investment that would not be viable without subsidization. Unless significant positive externalities can be shown, such investments may be undesirable, as they may cause a serious misallocation of resources.

Another downside of debt-for-equity swaps is the possible lack of transparency of the investment operations. Because of the various subsidy elements involved, the pricing of the assets offered for sale—usually in the context of the privatization of a state-owned enterprise—becomes less transparent. Insufficient clarity on subsidization and pricing undermines the integrity of the government budget of the debtor country, and may raise governance concerns. To address these problems, governments involved in debt swaps should maintain transparent bidding procedures, and ensure that the fiscal and quasi-fiscal cost of subsidization is properly reflected in the government accounts.

Large-scale debt-for-equity swaps can have destabilizing macroeconomic effects in the debtor country, especially if monetary and fiscal policies do not sufficiently take into account the demand effects of higher foreign-financed investment. For instance, if the inward investment is associated with investment-related domestic spending financed through large direct and indirect subsidies, inflationary pressures may arise. While such a policy may be objectionable for the reasons mentioned above, it also raises issues of macroeconomic management. The appropriate policy response in such situations would be to reduce government expenditure in other areas or raise taxes to offset the fiscal impulse resulting from the subsidies. This scenario emphasizes, however, the potential distortionary impact of debt-for-equity swaps. Indeed, the reduction in expenditure required to maintain macroeconomic balance may disadvantage efforts to promote economic growth and poverty reduction, especially if the cuts affect domestic spending on health, education, or capital projects. Thus, economic benefits from the investment generated by debt-for-equity swaps may be more than offset by the associated crowding-out effects. "Round-tripping" and "additionality" are two related problems that may also offset some of the debtor country's gains from debt-swap operations. Round-tripping occurs when in a debt-equity swap a firm finds a way to take an equivalent amount of capital out of the debtor country. After swapping debt for equity, an investor then sells the equity and withdraws the proceeds from the country. In this case, the debt-equity swap becomes equivalent to a buyback on the secondary market, probably at less than the full discount. Additionality becomes a problem if a debt-equity swap finances an investment that would have taken place in any case. Had the foreign firm carried out the investment without a swap, it would have brought foreign exchange to the central bank to exchange for local currency with which to make the investment.

To protect against round-tripping, a government can impose a lockup period on the investor's ability to repatriate the capital portion of the investment and require that the local firm pays dividends only out of profits earned. Instead of handing over the money to the investor, the government can also directly disburse money to the domestic suppliers, contractors, and creditors of the firm. To counter the problems of additionality, the government can require the investor to provide new money to be able to participate in the program.

Debt Swaps by Paris Club Creditors

Until the early 1990s nearly all the debt swaps were carried out by private creditors. There were hardly any swaps involving official bilateral creditors, including ODA and commercial debt guaranteed by creditor governments or by their export credit agencies. Explicit provisions allowing official bilateral creditors to engage in swaps were first introduced in Paris Club rescheduling agreements in September 1990 for lower middle-income countries. According to these terms, $10 million or 10 percent of concerned commercial credits per creditor, whichever was higher, could be converted on a purely voluntary and bilateral basis in the form of debt-for-equity, debt-for-aid or development, debt-for-nature, and other debt-for-local-currency operations. No restriction was placed on the amount of ODA loans that could be swapped. Subsequently, in December 1991, these provisions were extended to low-income countries. In June 1996, Paris Club creditors agreed to raise the amount of commercial debt that could be swapped to the greater of 20 percent of concerned commercial credits outstanding, or SDR 15–30 million per creditor.

Paris Club creditors swapped $4.5 billion claims on developing countries during the period 1991–April 2000. In the same period, debt swaps amounted to about 10 percent of the average outstanding debt stock owed by debtor countries to the creditor countries implementing the swaps. Debt swap activity averaged $500 million per year during the 1991–99 period and peaked in 1994 and 1998 at nearly $1 billion (Table A4 and Figure A3) as a result of large debt swaps with Egypt in 1994, and Peru and Morocco in 1998. Typically, the terms of swaps

Table A4. Evolution of Debt Swaps by Paris Club Creditors, 1991–April 2000

	1991	1992	1993	1994	1995	1996	1997	1998	1999	Jan–Apr 2000	Total
					(Millions of U.S. dollars)						
Total debt swaps	134	239	754	982	696	426	105	932	246	19	4,532
Debt-for-equity swaps	74	94	382	780	246	80	21	511	46	—	2,236
Debt-for-nature/aid swaps	60	145	304	202	450	345	76	113	199	19	1,913
Other[1]	—	—	68	—	—	—	8	308	—	—	383
					(Percent of total)						
Debt-equity swap	55	39	51	79	35	19	20	55	19	—	49
Debt-for-nature/aid swaps	45	61	40	21	65	81	73	12	81	100	42
Other[1]	—	—	9	—	—	—	7	33	—	—	8

Source: Paris Club Secretariat.

[1]Other swaps include swaps for health, nutrition, water, sanitation, environmental child survival programs, industry and export promotion, and technical equipment for educational purposes. All amounts are at nominal value of the original debt.

included a purchase price and a rate of redemption in local currency of less than half the face value of the debt. Swaps were implemented both outside and within the context of Paris Club rescheduling agreements.

Swap activity has been a function of debt exposure, the creditor country's policy towards swaps including whether its domestic laws permitted participation in swap activity, and the availability of attractive assets in debtor countries. In all, 13 creditor countries and 37 debtor countries participated in swaps in the period covered (Table A5). The most active creditor countries were France ($1.4 billion) and Switzerland ($0.9 billion). While the overall amounts were much smaller, Belgium was also very active and swapped debt with 13 debtor countries—thereby reducing the cost of administering small claims.

On the debtor side, Egypt was by far the most active country swapping debt of nearly $1.6 billion, followed by Morocco ($526 million), Peru ($455 million), and Côte d'Ivoire ($326 million). About half of the debtor countries (6 out of 34) implemented swaps with only one creditor country. However, Egypt swapped debt with eight creditor countries, Peru and Tanzania with six creditor countries each, and Jordan and Poland with five creditor countries each.

In terms of the type of debt swapped, nearly three-fourths ($3.2 billion) related to commercial (non-ODA) debt (Table A6). Australia, Belgium, Italy, Sweden, Switzerland, and the United Kingdom swapped only commercial debt, and France and Finland mostly so. Canada, Germany, and the Netherlands swapped mainly ODA debt.

Regarding the type of swap arrangements entered into by creditor countries, debt-equity and debt-for-nature/aid swaps accounted, in terms of the amounts involved, for 50 percent and 40 percent, respectively, of total swaps (Table A7). Australia, Spain, and the United Kingdom implemented exclusively debt-equity swaps, and France and Sweden mostly so. In contrast, all the debt swapped by Canada, Finland, Germany, the Netherlands, Switzerland, and the United States was in the form of debt-for-nature/aid swaps or other forms. Belgium had a somewhat even distribution of debt swapped between debt-equity and debt-for-nature/aid swap. In terms of their share of the total, debt-for-nature/aid rose from close to 25 percent in 1991 to about 80 percent in 1999 (Figure A3). Debt-for-nature/aid swaps are more likely to involve an element of debt forgiveness by the creditors than debt-for-equity swaps.

Austria, Denmark, Italy, Japan, and Norway have not implemented any debt swaps due to the absence of a legal basis to do so in their domestic legislation. In March 1998, Italy adopted legislation that would permit swap operations.

In the case of the United States, provisions for debt swaps and buybacks of nonconcessional

Eximbank and Commodity Credit Corporation export credit assets was included in the Enterprise for the Americas Initiative (EAI) announced in June 1990. It aimed to enhance development prospects through action in the areas of trade, investment, and debt. Under the EAI, debts owed by developing countries in the Western Hemisphere to the U.S. government could be reduced provided that the country (i) undertook macroeconomic and structural reforms; (ii) liberalized its investment regime; and (iii) concluded a debt restructuring agreement with its commercial bank creditors. The EAI provided for a reduction of concessional debts, including loans disbursed under programs of food assistance (Public Law 480) and development assistance from the Agency for International Development (AID). Countries benefiting from debt reductions could make interest payments on the remaining debt in local currency if they negotiated "Framework Agreements" under which these resources would be committed to environmental or child development projects.[62] The remaining principal was to be repaid in U.S. dollars. In addition, some part of the nonconcessional debt owed to U.S. Eximbank and the Commodity Credit Corporation might either be bought back by the debtor or used to facilitate debt-for-equity or debt-for-nature/aid swaps.

Under the EAI, a total of $1.2 billion in debt was forgiven for Argentina, Bolivia, Chile, Colombia, El Salvador, Jamaica, Peru, and Uruguay, during fiscal years 1991–98, and as a result of this debt reduction an additional $331 million in interest payments was forgiven in conjunction with commitments to make equivalent local currency payments for environmental and child development programs. In July 1998, building upon the EAI, the United States Congress enacted the "Tropical Forest Conservation Act of 1998" (see Box A2).

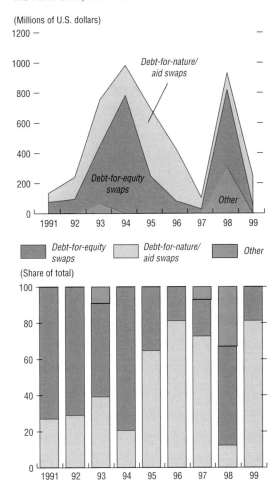

Figure A3. Evolution of Debt Swaps in the Context of the Paris Club, 1991–99

(Millions of U.S. dollars)

Debt-for-nature/aid swaps

Debt-for-equity swaps

Other

Debt-for-equity swaps Debt-for-nature/aid swaps Other

(Share of total)

Sources: Paris Club, and IMF staff estimates.

---

[62]Only the amounts related to such local currency payments are included in the data on swaps presented in this appendix.

Table A5. Debt Swaps by Paris Club Creditors, 1991–April 2000
By Creditor and Debtor Country Distribution

Creditors:	Australia	Belgium	Canada	Finland	France	Germany	Italy	Netherlands	Spain	Sweden	Switzerland	UK	USA[1]	Total swaps (US$ millions)	Number of creditor countries
Argentina													x	3	1
Benin		x												14	1
Bolivia		x				x					x		x	173	4
Bulgaria											x			20	1
Cameroon		x												15	1
Chile								x					x	21	2
Colombia			x										x	58	2
Congo, Rep.of		x												18	1
Costa Rica			x					x						37	2
Côte d'Ivoire		x									x			326	2
Ecuador											x			45	1
Egypt	x	x			x	x			x	x	x	x		1,648	8
El Salvador										x		x	x	51	2
Guinea Bissau											x			14	1
Guinea		x									x			11	2
Honduras			x		x	x					x			89	4
Jamaica			x					x						26	2
Jordan				x	x	x				x	x			169	5
Madagascar								x						3	1
Mauritania														—	0
Morocco					x				x					526	2
Mozambique			x			x			x			x		37	4
Nicaragua									x					18	1
Nigeria		x								x		x		75	3
Pakistan								x						3	1
Peru			x	x		x				x	x		x	455	6
Philippines				x		x					x			64	3
Poland				x	x		x			x	x			166	5
Russian Fed.						x								127	1
Senegal											x			17	1
Suriname		x												1	1
Syria									x					43	1
Tanzania		x			x	x				x	x	x		140	6
Tunisia								x						26	1
Uruguay													x	6	1
Vietnam		x				x								76	2
Zambia		x												10	1
Total	26	406	124	171	1,406	424	33	54	393	90	922	153	331	4,532	

Source: Paris Club.
[1] Over 1991–93, all swapped debts were concessional loans provided under PL–480 and USAID, and all swaps were debt-for-nature and aid swaps.

Table A6. Debt Swaps with Paris Club Creditors, 1991–April 2000
by Type of Debt

| | Type of Debt[1] | | | | |
	ODA	Non-ODA	Total	ODA	Non-ODA
	(Millions of U.S. dollars)			(Percent of total)	
Australia	—	26	26	. . .	. . .
Belgium	—	406	406	. . .	. . .
Canada	124	—	124	100.0	—
Finland	27	144	171	15.7	84.3
France	297	1,109	1,406	21.1	78.9
Germany	344	80	424	81.1	18.9
Italy	—	33	33	. . .	. . .
The Netherlands	47	7	54	87.0	13.0
Spain	190	203	393	48.2	51.8
Sweden	—	90	90	. . .	. . .
Switzerland	—	922	922	. . .	. . .
UK	—	153	153	. . .	. . .
USA[2]	177	145	322	55.0	45.0
Total	**1,027**	**3,174**	**4,523**	**22.7**	**77.3**

Source: Paris Club Secretariat.
[1]All amounts are at face/nominal value of the original debt.
[2]All debts swapped were concessional loans provided under PL-480 and USAID and all swaps were debt-for-nature and aid swaps.

Table A7. Debt Swaps by Paris Club Creditors, 1991–April 2000
by Type of Swaps

Creditors	Equity	Nature/Aid	Other	Total	Equity	Nature/Aid	Other
	(Millions of U.S. dollars)[1]				(Percent of total)		
Australia	26	—	—	26	100	—	—
Belgium	184	222	—	406	45	55	—
Canada	—	124	—	124	—	100	—
Finland	—	40	131	171	—	23	77
France	1,248	158	—	1,406	89	11	—
Germany	160	264	—	424	38	62	—
Italy	—	33	—	33	—	100	—
The Netherlands	—	54	—	54	—	100	—
Spain	393	—	—	393	100	—	—
Sweden	72	18	—	90	80	20	—
Switzerland	—	846	76	922	—	92	8
UK	153	—	—	153	100	—	—
USA[2]	—	154	177	331	—	47	53
Total	**2,236**	**1,913**	**383**	**4,532**	**49**	**42**	**8**

Source: Paris Club.
[1]All amounts are at face/nominal value of the original debt.
[2]All swapped debts were concessional loans provided under PL-480 and USAID and all swaps were debt-for-nature and aid swaps.

Box A2. U.S. Tropical Forest Conservation Act of 1998

The Act allows low- and middle-income countries containing tropical forests to engage in debt buybacks or in debt-for-nature swaps making use of concessional debt owed to the United States.[1] Under the act, a **Tropical Forest Facility** was established; to be eligible to benefit from this facility the developing country should have a bilateral investment treaty with the United States and an investment reform program supported by the World Bank or the Inter-American Development Bank. The U.S. government will allow the sale, reduction, cancellation, or partial cancellation of the eligible debt to a third party (after consulting the debtor government) for the purpose of facilitating debt-for-nature swaps. For engaging in debt-for-nature swaps, the purchaser of the debt will have to present plans that are satisfactory to the U.S. government, for using the loan. The debtor government will also be allowed to buy back its eligible debt provided it is willing to devote, in local currency, 40 percent of the purchase price or the difference between the face value of the loan and the purchase price, whichever is less, to support activities to preserve and restore tropical forests.

[1]For fiscal year 1999 and fiscal year 2000, the following countries are eligible if they meet the other criteria as given in the law: Bolivia, Brazil, Ecuador, Guyana, Côte d'Ivoire, Liberia, Madagascar, Indonesia, Papua New Guinea, Peru, and the Philippines.

ADF. Asian Development Fund.

AfDB. African Development Bank.

AfDF. African Development Fund.

Agreed Minute. Paris Club document detailing the terms of a rescheduling between creditors and the debtor. It specifies the coverage of debt service payments (types of debt treated), the cutoff date, the consolidation period (in the case of a flow rescheduling), the proportion of payments to be rescheduled, the provisions regarding any down payment, and the repayment schedules for rescheduled and deferred debt. Representatives in the Paris Club commit to recommending these terms to their governments for the bilateral agreements negotiated with the debtor government that implements the Agreed Minute. Paris Club creditors will only agree to reschedulings with countries that have an IMF upper credit tranche arrangement (Stand-By Arrangement, or Extended Fund Facility), a Poverty Reduction and Growth Facility arrangement, or a Rights Accumulation Program.

Arrears. Unpaid or overdue payments. In the context of export credits, arrears are overdue payments by borrowers that have not yet resulted in claims on export credit agencies.

AsDB. Asian Development Bank.

BIS. Bank for International Settlements.

Berne Union (International Union of Credit and Investment Insurers). An association, founded in 1934, of export credit insurance agencies, all participating as insurers and not as representatives of their governments. The main purposes of the Union are to work for sound principles of export credit insurance and maintenance of discipline in the terms of credit in international trade. To this end, members exchange information and furnish the Union with information on their activities, consult with each other on a continuing basis, and cooperate closely.

Bilateral Paris Club agreements. Agreements reached bilaterally between the debtor country and agencies in each of the creditor countries participating in a Paris Club rescheduling. These agreements put into effect the debt restructuring set forth in the Agreed Minute and are legally the equivalent of new loan agreements.

Bilateral official creditors. The creditors are governments. Their claims are loans extended, insured, or guaranteed by governments or official agencies, such as export credit agencies. Certain official creditors participate in debt reschedulings under the aegis of the Paris Club.

Bilateral deadline. In the context of Paris Club reschedulings, the date by which all bilateral agreements must be concluded. It is set in the Agreed Minute and is typically around six months after conclusion of the Agreed Minute, but it can be extended upon request.

Brady Plan. Approach adopted in the late 1980s to restructure debt to commercial banks that emphasizes voluntary market-based debt and debt service reduction operations (DDSR). The main feature of the DDSR operations is the menu of options offered to creditors, which consists of some combination of a buyback at a significant discount, and the issuance of "Brady bonds" by the debtor country in exchange for banks' claims. Such operations complement countries' efforts to restore external viability through the adoption of medium-term structural adjustment programs supported by the IMF and other multilateral and official bilateral creditors.

Buyback. The purchase by a debtor of its own debt, usually at a substantial discount. The debtor reduces its obligations while the creditor receives a once-and-for-all payment.

Buyers' credit. A financial arrangement in which a bank or financial institution, or an export credit agency in the exporting country, extends a loan directly to a foreign buyer or to a bank in the importing country to finance the purchase of goods and services from the exporting country.

CABEI. Central American Bank for Economic Integration.

CAF. Corporación Andina de Fomento.

Cancellation of a loan. An agreed reduction in the undisbursed balance of a loan commitment.

Capitalized interest. Scheduled interest payments that are converted, through an agreement made with the creditor, into debt. Rescheduling agreements sometimes provide for the capitalization (of some percentage) of interest due during the consolidation period.

Capitalization of moratorium interest option. Option under concessional Paris Club reschedulings where creditors effect the required NPV debt relief through a reduction in the applicable interest rate (but a lower reduction than in the debt service reduction option) and with a partial capitalization of moratorium interest. This option is chosen by creditors only rarely (see concessional rescheduling).

Claims payments. Payments made to exporters or banks, after the claims-waiting period, by an export credit agency on insured or guaranteed loans, when the original borrower or borrowing-country guarantor fails to pay. This is recorded by the agencies as an unrecovered claim.

Claims-waiting period. The period that exporters or banks must wait after arrears occur before the export credit agency will pay on the corresponding claim.

Cofinancing. The joint or parallel financing of programs or projects through loans or grants to developing countries provided by commercial banks, export credit agencies, or other official institutions in association with other agencies or banks, or the World Bank and other multilateral financial institutions.

Cologne terms. See concessional rescheduling.

Commercial credit. In the context of the Paris Club, loans originally extended on terms that do not qualify as ODA credits. These are typically export credits on market terms or have a relatively small grant element.

Commercial Interest Reference Rates (CIRRs). A set of currency-specific interest rates for major OECD countries. These rates are determined monthly based on the secondary market yield on government bonds.

Commercial risk. In the context of export credits, the risk of nonpayment by a nonsovereign or private sector buyer or borrower in his home currency arising from default, insolvency, and/or failure to take up goods that have been shipped according to the supply contract (contrasted with transfer risk arising from an inability to convert local currency into the currency in which the debt is denominated, or broader political risk).

Commitment. In the context of export credits, a contractual obligation by an export credit agency to lend, guarantee, or insure resources under specified financial terms and conditions and for specified purposes for the benefit of an importer. In the context of data reported by export credit agencies, the total amount of loans excluding amounts that are in arrears or on which claims have been paid, usually includes principal and contractual interest payable by the importing country on disbursed and undisbursed credits, and sometimes includes not only liabilities of the agency but also uninsured parts of the loan. Therefore, reported commitments are almost always larger than the face value of the loan, and sometimes larger than the agency's total exposure.

Commitment charge (or fee). This is the charge made for holding available the undisbursed balance of a loan commitment. Typically it is a fixed rate charge (for example, 1.5 percent per annum) calculated on the basis of the undisbursed balance.

Comparable treatment. An understanding in a debt restructuring agreement with the Paris Club creditors that the debtor will secure at least equivalent debt relief from other creditors.

Completion point. In the context of the HIPC Initiative, a point at which the country concerned completes a set of structural adjustment and poverty reduction measures in the context of IMF- and World Bank-supported programs after reaching the decision point (see decision point) and the debt relief committed by the international community becomes irrevocable.

Concessionality level. See grant element.

Concessional rescheduling. Rescheduling of debt with partial debt reduction. In the context of the Paris Club, concessional rescheduling terms have been granted to low-income countries since October 1988 with a reduction in the net present value (NPV) of eligible debt of up to one-third (Toronto terms); since December 1991 with an NPV reduction of up to half (London terms or "enhanced concessions" or "enhanced Toronto" terms); and since January 1995 with an NPV reduction of up to two-thirds (Naples terms). In the context of the HIPC Initiative, creditors agreed in November 1996 to increase the NPV reduction up to 80 percent (Lyon terms). In November 1999, the concessionality of such debt relief operations was increased to 90 percent debt reduction in NPV terms (Cologne terms). Such reschedulings can be in the form of flow reschedulings or stock-of-debt operations. While the terms (grace period and maturity) are standard, creditors can choose from a menu of options to implement the debt relief. For full details, see Section V, Table 5.3.

Consensus. See OECD Consensus.

Consolidated amounts or consolidated debt. The debt service payments and arrears, or debt stock, rescheduled under a Paris Club rescheduling agreement.

Consolidation period. In Paris Club rescheduling agreements, the period in which debt service payments to be rescheduled (the "current maturities consolidated") fall due. The beginning of the consolidation period may precede, coincide with, or come after the date of the Agreed Minute. The end of the consolidation period is generally the end of the month in which the IMF arrangement, on the basis of which the rescheduling takes place, expires.

Cover. Provision of export credit guarantee/insurance against risks of payments delays or non-payments relating to export transactions. Cover is usually, though not always, provided both for commercial risk and for political risk. In most cases, cover is not provided for the full value of future debt service payments; the percentage of cover typically is between 90 and 95 percent. (See also quantitative limits.)

Coverage. In the context of rescheduling agreements, the debt service or arrears rescheduled. Comprehensive coverage implies the inclusion of most or all eligible debt service and arrears.

Credit guarantee. Commitment by an export credit agency to reimburse a lender if the borrower fails to repay a loan. The lender pays a guarantee fee. While guarantees could be unconditional, they usually have conditions attached to them, so that in practice there is little distinction between credits that are guaranteed and credits that are subject to insurance.

Credit insurance. The main business of most export credit agencies is insurance of finance provided by exporters or commercial creditors (though some major agencies lend on their own account). Insurance policies provide for the export credit agency to reimburse the lender for losses up to a certain percentage of the credit covered and under certain conditions. Lenders or exporters pay a premium to the export credit agency. Insurance policies typically protect the lender against political or transfer risks in the borrowing country that prevent the remittance of debt service payments.

Current maturities. In the context of rescheduling agreements, principal and interest payments falling due in the consolidation period.

Cutoff date. The date (established at the time of a country's first Paris Club rescheduling) before which loans must have been contracted in order for their debt service to be eligible for rescheduling. New loans extended after the cutoff date are protected from future rescheduling (subordination strategy). In exceptional cases, arrears on post-cutoff date debt can be deferred over short periods of time in rescheduling agreements.

De minimis creditors (or clause). Minor creditors that are exempted from debt restructuring to simplify implementation of the Paris Club rescheduling agreements. Their claims are payable in full as they fall due. An exposure limit defining a minor creditor is included in each Agreed Minute, typically ranging from SDR 250,000 to SDR 1 million of consolidated debt.

Debt and debt service reduction (DDSR) operations. Debt restructuring agreements typically between sovereign states and consortia of commercial bank creditors involving a combination of buyback, and exchange of eligible commercial debt for financial instruments at a substantial discount (simple cash buyback) or for new bonds featuring a net present value reduction. In some instances, the principal portion of new financial instruments is fully collateralized with U.S. Treasury zero-coupon bonds, while interest obligations are also partially secured. DDSR agreements are characterized by a "menu approach," allowing individual creditors to select from among several DDSR options. Under the Brady Plan of March 1989, some of these arrangements have been supported by loans from official creditors.

Debt-equity swap. An arrangement that results in the exchange of debt claims, usually at a discount, for equity in an enterprise. An investor purchases the title to a foreign currency denominated debt in a secondary market at a substantial discount. Under the debt-equity swap program, the debtor country government will exchange the debt for local currency. The investor will then carry out an approved equity investment project. The difference between the face value and the market value of the debt provides an incentive to the investor.

Debt-for-debt swap. Such swaps involve a change of creditor without otherwise changing the terms of repayment of their respective loans. They may involve external or domestic creditors (see Box A1, pages 67–68).

Debt-for-development swap. Financing part of a development project by the exchange of a foreign currency denominated debt for local currency, typically at a substantial discount. The process normally involves a foreign nongovernmental organization (NGO), which purchases the debt from the original creditor at a substantial discount using its own foreign currency resources, and then resells it to the debtor country government for the local currency equivalent (resulting in a further discount). The NGO in turn spends the money on a development project, previously agreed upon with the debtor country government.

Debt-for-local-currency swap. Local residents, instead of a foreign investor, buy their own currency's debt in the secondary market using funds they hold abroad or foreign currency acquired in the exchange market. These swaps are designed primarily for the repatriation of flight capital.

Debt-for-nature swap. Similar to a debt-for-development swap, except that the funds are used for projects that improve the environment.

Debt forgiveness or debt reduction. The extinction of a debt, in whole or in part, by agreement between debtor and creditor. Debt reduction in the context of concessional reschedulings from the Paris Club is applied to the net present value of eligible debt.

Debt reduction option. Option under concessional Paris Club reschedulings where creditors effect the required debt relief in net present value terms through a reduction of the principal of the consolidated amount. A commercial interest rate and standard repayment terms apply to the remaining amounts (see concessional reschedulings). For precise terms see Section V.

Debt refinancing. Procedure by which overdue payments or future debt-service obligations on an officially-supported export credit are paid off using a new "refinancing" loan. The refinancing loan can be extended by the export credit agency, by a governmental institution, or by a commercial bank, and in the latter case will carry the guarantee of the export credit agency.

Debt rescheduling. See rescheduling.

Debt restructuring. Any action by a creditor that alters the terms established for repayment of debt in a manner that provides for smaller nearterm debt service obligations (debt relief). This includes rescheduling, refinancing, debt and debt service reduction operations, buybacks, and forgiveness.

Debt service(-to-exports) ratio. A key indicator of a country's debt burden. Scheduled debt service (interest and principal payments due) during a year expressed as a percentage of exports (typically of goods and nonfactor services) for that year.

Debt service reduction option. Option under concessional Paris Club reschedulings where creditors effect the required debt relief in net present value terms through a reduction in the applicable interest rate (see concessional reschedulings). For precise terms, see Section V, Table 5.2.

Debt sustainability. As defined in the context of the enhanced HIPC Initiative, the position of a country when the net present value (NPV) of (public and publicly guaranteed) debt-to-exports is below 150 percent. For highly open economies (indicated by an exports-to-GDP ratio of at least 30 percent) making a strong fiscal effort (expressed by a fiscal revenue-to-GDP ratio of at least 15 percent) the threshold is equivalent to a NPV of debt-to-revenue ratio of 250 percent.

Debt sustainability analysis (DSA). A study of a country's long-term debt situation jointly undertaken by the staffs of the IMF and the World Bank and the country concerned, in consultation with creditors. A country's eligibility for support under the HIPC Initiative is determined on the basis of such an analysis.

Debtor Reporting System (DRS). Statistical reporting system maintained by the World Bank to monitor the debt of developing countries on the basis of reports from debtor countries. Basis for the annual World Bank report, *Global Development Finance* (formerly, *World Debt Tables*).

Decision point. In the context of the HIPC Initiative, point at which a country's eligibility for assistance under the HIPC Initiative is determined based on the debt sustainability analysis. In order to reach a decision point, a country needs to establish a credible track record in the context of an IMF- and World Bank-supported program, while receiving a flow rescheduling on Naples terms from Paris Club creditors and comparable treatment from other official bilateral and commercial creditors. The international community enters into a commitment at the decision point to deliver assistance at the completion point provided the debtor adheres to its policy commitments.

Deferred payments. In the context of Paris Club reschedulings, obligations that are not consolidated but postponed nonconcessionally, usually for a short period of time, as specified in the Agreed Minute.

Development Assistance Committee (DAC) of the OECD. Established in 1960 as the Development Assistance Group with the objective to expand the volume of resources made available to the developing countries and to improve their effectiveness. The DAC periodically reviews both the amount and nature of its members' contributions to aid programs, both bilateral and multilateral. The DAC does not disburse assistance funds directly but is concerned instead with the promotion of increased assistance efforts by its members. The members of the DAC are Australia, Austria, Belgium, Canada, Denmark, Finland, France, Germany, Ireland, Italy, Japan, Luxembourg, the Netherlands, New Zealand, Norway, Portugal, Spain, Sweden, Switzerland, the United Kingdom, the United States, and the Commission of the European Communities.

EDF. European Development Fund.

Effectively rescheduled debt. The proportion of total payments covered by a rescheduling agreement that is rescheduled or deferred until after the consolidation period.

EIB. European Investment Bank.

Eligible debt or debt service. In the context of the Paris Club, debt that can be rescheduled, namely debt contracted before the cutoff date with maturities of one year or longer.

Enhanced concessions (or enhanced Toronto terms). See concessional rescheduling.

Enhanced Structural Adjustment Facility (ESAF). See Structural Adjustment Facility (SAF).

Escrow accounts. Accounts in offshore banks (outside the debtor country) through which a portion of the export proceeds of a debtor is channeled to cover future debt service payments. Creditors thus obtain extra security for their loans and effective priority on debt service.

EU. European Union.

Export credit. A loan extended to finance a specific purchase of goods or services from within the creditor country. Export credits extended by the supplier of goods are known as suppliers credits; export credits extended by the supplier's bank are known as buyers credits. (See also officially supported export credits.)

Exposure. In the context of export credits, the total amount of debt of a country held by an export credit agency, including commitments, arrears, and unrecovered claims. Implicitly, a measure of the total possible financial cost to the agency of a complete default by the borrowing country.

Extended Fund Facility (EFF). An IMF lending facility established in 1974 to assist member countries in overcoming balance of payments problems that stem largely from structural problems and require a longer period of adjustment. A member requesting an extended arrangement outlines its objectives and policies for the whole period of the arrangement (typically three years)

and presents a detailed statement each year of the policies and measures to be pursued over the next 12 months. The phasing and performance criteria are comparable to those of Stand-By Arrangements, although phasing on a semiannual basis is possible. Countries must repay EFF resources over 10 years including a grace period of 4½ years (see Stand-By Arrangement).

Flow rescheduling. In the context of the Paris Club, the rescheduling of specified debt service falling due during the consolidation period, and, in some cases, of specified arrears outstanding at the beginning of the consolidation period (see stock-of-debt operation).

Goodwill clause. Clause used in Paris Club agreements under which creditors agree in principle, but without commitment, to consider favorably subsequent debt relief agreements for a debtor country that remains in compliance with the rescheduling agreement as well as its IMF arrangement and that has sought comparable debt relief from other creditors. The clause can be for a future flow rescheduling or a stock-of-debt operation.

Grace period and maturity. During the grace period of a loan, no principal repayments (amortization) need to be made, only interest payments are due. Maturity refers to the total repayment period, including the grace period. In the context of Paris Club reschedulings, periods until the first and last payment dates are measured typically from the mid-point of the consolidation period.

Graduated payments (or "blended payments"). In the context of Paris Club rescheduling, the term refers to a repayment schedule where principal repayments (and therefore total payments) gradually increase over the repayment period reflecting an expected improvement in the repayment capacity of a debtor country. Creditors have made increasing use of the graduated payments replacing flat payment schedules where equal amounts of principal repayments were made over the repayment period: from the creditor perspective, they provide for principal repayments starting earlier and from the debtor perspective, they avoid a large jump in debt service falling due.

Grant element. Measure of concessionality of a loan, calculated as the difference between the face value of the loan and the sum of the discounted future debt service payments to be made by the borrower expressed as a percentage of the face value of the loan.

Grant-like flows. Transactions involving the sale of commodities against payment in the recipient country's currency or loans in a foreign currency repayable in the recipient country's currency. These transactions are treated as grants in the OECD/DAC statistics. They are, nevertheless, counted as external debt, since the creditor is nonresident.

Heavily Indebted Poor Countries (HIPCs). Group of 41 developing countries identified for analytical purposes in 1995: includes 32 countries with a 1993 GNP per capita of $695 or less and 1993 present value of debt to exports higher than 220 percent or present value of debt to GNP higher than 80 percent (severely indebted low-income countries in the World Bank classification). Also includes 9 countries that have received concessional reschedulings from Paris Club creditors (or are potentially eligible for such rescheduling).

Helsinki package. Agreement reached in 1978 by OECD participants of the Consensus limiting the use of tied-aid credits in certain countries to projects that would not be commercially viable without an aid element. The agreement also set up mechanisms for implementing the new rules. (See OECD Consensus.)

HIPC Initiative—Debt Initiative for Heavily Indebted Poor Countries. Framework for action to resolve the external debt problems of heavily indebted poor countries (HIPCs) that was developed jointly by the IMF and the World Bank and was adopted in 1996 and revised in 1999. The Initiative envisages comprehensive action by the international financial community, including multilateral institutions, to assist eligi-

ble HIPCs achieve debt sustainability, provided a country builds a track record of strong policy performance.

HIPC Trust Fund. Trust Fund administered by IDA to provide debt relief through grants to eligible HIPCs on debt owed to participating multilaterals. It will either prepay, or purchase a portion of the debt owed to a multilateral creditor and cancel such debt, or pay debt service as it comes due. The HIPC Trust Fund receives contributions from participating multilateral creditors and from bilateral donors. Contributions can be earmarked for debt owed by a particular debtor or to a particular multilateral creditor. Donors can also provide contributions to an unallocated pool and would participate in decisions regarding the use of these unallocated funds. The Trust Fund allows multilateral creditors to participate in the Trust Fund in ways consistent with their financial policies and aims to address the resource constraints for certain multilateral creditors (see also PRGF-HIPC Trust).

Houston terms. See lower-middle-income country terms.

IBRD. International Bank for Reconstruction and Development.

ICSID. International Center for the Settlement of Investment Disputes.

IDB. Inter-American Development Bank.

IFAD. International Fund for Agricultural Development.

IFC. International Finance Corporation.

IMF arrangement. Agreement between the IMF and a member-country based on which the IMF provides financial assistance to a member country seeking to redress balance of payments problems and to help cushion the impact of adjustment. Nonconcessional resources are provided mainly under Stand-By Arrangements (SBA) and the Extended Fund Facility (EFF), and concessional resources are provided under the Poverty Reduction and Growth Facility (PRGF).

Implementing agreements. See bilateral agreements.

Interest rate swap. An agreement to swap the debt-servicing liability of a loan with a fixed interest rate for that of a loan with a variable interest rate. For example, a government of a developing country may be able to borrow at comparatively better terms at variable rates than at fixed rates, while for an enterprise in an industrialized country the inverse may be true. As each may prefer its liabilities in the other form, they may therefore arrange a swap. Normally, the differential in the rates is insured with a broker to protect the more sound borrower.

International Development Association (IDA). IDA is the concessional lending arm of the World Bank Group. IDA assistance is available to low-income member countries.

Late interest. Interest accrued on principal and interest in arrears.

London Club. A group of commercial banks that join together to negotiate the restructuring of their claims against a particular sovereign debtor. There is no organizational framework for the London Club comparable to that of the Paris Club.

London terms. See concessional rescheduling.

Long-maturities option. In the context of the Paris Club, a nonconcessional option in concessional reschedulings under which the consolidated amount is rescheduled over a long period of time but without a reduction in the net present value of the debt.

Low-income countries. In the context of the Paris Club, countries eligible to receive concessional terms. The Paris Club decides eligibility on a case-by-case basis, but these typically include countries eligible to receive only highly concessional credits from the IDA ("IDA-only countries").

Lower-middle-income country terms (LMIC). In the context of the Paris Club, refers to the rescheduling terms granted, since September 1990, to lower-middle-income countries. These terms are nonconcessional, and provided originally for flat repayment schedules, but in recent years often graduated payment schedules have been agreed for commercial credits with up to 18-year maturities, including a grace period of up to 8 years. ODA credits are rescheduled over 20 years including a grace period of up to 10 years. This set of rescheduling terms also includes the limited use of debt swaps on a voluntary basis. In 2000, lower-middle-income countries were countries with a per capita GNP between $756 and $2,995.

Lyon terms. See concessional rescheduling.

Maturity. Grace period plus repayment period. See grace period and maturity.

Middle-income countries. In the context of the Paris Club, countries not considered lower-middle-income or low-income. These countries receive nonconcessional rescheduling terms, originally with flat repayment schedules, but since the 1990s increasingly with graduated payment schedules that have a maturity of up to 18 years and a grace period of 2–3 years for commercial credits. Official development assistance credits are rescheduled over 10 years, including a grace period of 5–6 years. In the context of the World Bank classification, middle-income countries are those with a GNP per capita income in 1999 of between US$756 and $9,265.

MIF. Multilateral Investment Fund.

MIGA. Multilateral Investment Guarantee Agency.

Mixed credits. Credits containing an aid element, either in the form of a grant or of a subsidized interest rate.

Moratorium interest. Interest charged on rescheduled debt. In the Paris Club, the moratorium interest rate is negotiated bilaterally by the borrowing country with each individual creditor and, therefore, differs from one creditor to the next. In the London Club, where all creditors are deemed to have access to funds at comparable rates, the moratorium interest rate applies equally to all rescheduled obligations under a given agreement.

Multilateral creditors. These creditors are multilateral institutions such as the IMF and the World Bank, and other multilateral development banks.

Multiyear rescheduling agreements (MYRA). An agreement granted by official creditors, that covers consolidation periods of two or more years in accordance with multiyear IMF arrangements such as EFF and PRGF. It is carried out through a succession of shorter consolidations (tranches) that are implemented after certain conditions specified in the Agreed Minute are satisfied. The conditions generally include full implementation to date of the rescheduling agreement and the continued implementation of the IMF arrangements.

Naples terms. See concessional rescheduling.

Net (capital) flows. Loan disbursements minus principal repayments during the same period.

Net present value (NPV) of debt. The discounted sum of all future debt service obligations (interest and principal) on existing debt. Whenever the interest rate on a loan is lower than the discount rate, the resulting NPV of debt is smaller than its face value, with the difference reflecting the grant element. The discount rates used in the context of the HIPC Initiative reflect market interest rates.

Net present value (NPV) of debt-to-exports ratio. Net present value (NPV) of debt as a percentage of exports (usually of goods and nonfactor services).

Net (capital) transfers. Loan disbursements minus debt service payments (principal repayment and interest) during the same period.

Nonconsolidated debt. This is debt that is wholly or partly excluded from rescheduling. It has to be repaid on the terms on which it was originally provided, unless creditors agree to defer it.

OECD. Organization for Economic Cooperation and Development.

OECD Consensus. Formally the "Arrangement on Guidelines for Officially Supported Export Credits," a framework of rules governing export credits agreed by members of the OECD's export credit group.

OECD Export Credit and Credit Guarantees Group, OECD Trade Committee. A forum in which 22 OECD member countries participate in the Arrangement on Guidelines for Officially Supported Export Credits (the Consensus). Turkey and Mexico also attend this Group as observers. Aside from coordinating export credit terms, the OECD Export Credit Group has also served as a forum for the exchange of information on debtor country situations and agencies' practices; at the meetings of the Group the governmental authorities of the agencies are represented.

Official creditors. Public sector lenders. Some are multilateral, namely, international financial institutions such as IMF, World Bank, and regional development banks. Others are bilateral, namely, agencies of individual governments (including central banks) such as export credit agencies.

Official development assistance (ODA). Flows of official financing defined by the OECD that meet the following test: (1) its main objective is the promotion of the economic development and welfare of the developing countries; and, (2) it is concessional in character and contains a grant element of at least 25 percent (using a fixed discount rate of 10 percent). ODA is provided to developing countries and to multilateral institutions by OECD/DAC members and other countries through their official agencies, including state and local governments, or by their executive agencies; ODA is also provided to developing countries by multilateral institutions. Lending by export credit agencies—with the pure purpose of export promotion—is excluded.

Official development finance (ODF). Total official flows to developing countries excluding officially supported export credits (the latter are regarded as primarily trade-promoting rather than development-oriented). Comprises official development assistance (ODA) and other official development finance flows.

Official export credit agency (ECA). An agency within a creditor country that provides loans, guarantees, or insurance to finance the specific purchase of goods for export (see officially supported export credits).

Officially supported export credits. Loans or credits to finance the export of goods and services for which an official export credit agency (ECA) in the creditor country provides guarantees, insurance, or direct financing. The financing element—as opposed to the guarantee/insurance element—may derive from various sources. It can be extended by an exporter (suppliers' credit), or through a commercial bank in the form of financial trade-related credit provided either to the supplier (also suppliers' credit) or to the importer (buyers' credit). It can also be extended directly by an ECA of the exporting countries, usually in the form of medium-term finance as a supplement to resources of the private sector, and generally for export promotion for capital equipment and large-scale, medium-term projects. Under OECD Consensus rules covering export credits with a duration of two years or more, up to 85 percent of the export contract value can be financed.

Other official development flows (other ODF). Development-oriented official flows that do not qualify as official development assistance (ODA). Bilateral "other" ODF includes mainly refinancing loans and the capitalization of interest in debt restructuring agreements.

Paris Club. Informal group of creditor governments that has met on a regular basis in Paris since 1956 to reschedule bilateral debts; the French Treasury provides the Secretariat. Creditors meet with a debtor country in order to reschedule its debts as part of the international support provided to a country that is experiencing debt-servicing difficulties and is pursuing an adjustment program supported by the IMF. The Paris Club does not have a fixed membership

and its meetings are open to all official creditors that accept its practices and procedures. The core creditors are mainly OECD member countries, but other creditors attend as relevant for a debtor country. Russia became a member in September 1997.

Political risk. The risk of borrower country government actions that prevent, or delay, the repayment of export credits. Many export credit agencies also include under political risk such events as war, civil war, revolution, or other disturbances that prevent the exporter from performing under the supply contract or the buyer from making payment. Some also include physical disasters such as cyclones, floods, or earthquakes.

Post-cutoff date debt. See cutoff date.

Poverty Reduction and Growth Facility (PRGF). In 1999, the PRGF replaced the ESAF as the IMF's concessional loan window.

Premium. In the context of export credits, the amount paid, usually in advance, by insured lenders as the price of the insurance. An important source of income for export credit agencies.

Previously rescheduled debt. Debt that has been rescheduled on a prior occasion. This type of debt was generally excluded from further rescheduling in both the Paris and the London Clubs until 1983. Since then, however, previously rescheduled debt frequently has been rescheduled again for countries facing acute payments difficulties.

PRGF-HIPC Trust. IMF's participation in the PRGF and the HIPC Initiative are administered through this Trust.

Quantitative (or cover) limits. Mechanisms by which export credit agencies restrict the amount of cover offered to a particular country. Could, for example, take the form of limits on the total cover for a country or on the amount of cover offered for individual transactions. The limit set is an important means of limiting exposure to countries considered to be risky.

Rights Accumulation Program (RAP). An IMF program of assistance established in 1990 whereby a member country with long overdue obligations to the IMF, while still in arrears, may accumulate "rights" toward a future disbursement from the IMF on the basis of a sustained performance under an IMF-monitored adjustment program. Countries incurring arrears to the IMF after end-1989 are not eligible for assistance under this program. Rights accumulation programs adhere to the macroeconomic and structural policy standards associated with programs supported by the EFF and PRGF, and performance is monitored, and rights accrue, quarterly.

Recoveries. Repayments made to export credit agencies by borrowing countries after agencies have paid out claims to exporters or banks on the loans concerned.

Refinancing. See debt refinancing.

Reinsurance. Reinsurance by export credit agencies of amounts originally insured by a private sector insurer or commercial bank (some large official agencies are also providing reinsurance for smaller official agencies). For example, a private insurer might keep the commercial risk of a loan on its own books, but seek reinsurance against specific political risks.

Repayment period. The period during which repayments under the financing are due to be made; this period usually starts after the end of performance under the commercial contract.

Rescheduling. Debt restructuring in which specified arrears and future debt service (falling due during the consolidation period) are consolidated and form a new loan with terms defined at the time of the rescheduling. Rescheduling debt is one means of providing a debtor with debt relief through a delay and, in the case of concessional rescheduling, a reduction in debt service obligations. For official bilateral creditors, the main forum for negotiating debt rescheduling is the Paris Club. Rescheduling is typically provided by the international financial community in order to support a debtor country's economic adjustment program.

Rescheduling agreement. An agreement between a creditor, or a group of creditors, and a debtor to reschedule debt. The agreement may also include other debt restructuring strategies such as write-offs or swaps.

Short-term commitments or credits. Commitments that provide for repayment within a short period, usually six months (though some export credit agencies define short-term credits as those with repayment terms of up to one or two years). Usually relating to sales of consumer goods and raw materials, and usually taking the form of policies for whole-turnover/comprehensive coverage. Short-term debt in the context of the Paris Club has a maturity of under and up to one year.

Special accounts. In the context of the Paris Club, deposits into special accounts were first introduced in 1983 for debtor countries that had a history of running into arrears. After the signing of the Agreed Minute, the debtor makes monthly deposits into an earmarked account at the central bank of one of the creditor countries. The deposit amounts are roughly equal to the moratorium interest that is expected to fall due on the rescheduled debt owed to all Paris Club creditors combined and any other payments falling due during the consolidation period. The debtor then draws on the deposited funds to make payments as soon as the bilateral agreements with the individual Paris Club creditors are signed and as other payments fall due.

Standard terms. See middle-income countries.

Stand-By Arrangement (SBA). An IMF lending facility established in 1952 through which a member country can use IMF financing up to a specified amount to overcome balance of payments difficulties of a short-term or cyclical character. Installments are normally phased on a quarterly basis, with their release conditional upon meeting performance criteria and the completion of periodic reviews. Performance criteria generally cover credit policy, government or public sector borrowing requirements, trade and payments restrictions, foreign borrowing, and reserve levels. These criteria allow both the member and the IMF to assess progress in policy implementation and may signal the need for further corrective policies. Stand-By Arrangements typically cover a 12 to 18 month period (although they can extend up to 3 years). Repayments are to be made over 5 years including a grace period of 3¼ years.

Standstill. This is an interim agreement between a debtor country and its commercial banking creditors that principal repayments of medium- and long-term debt will be deferred and that short term obligations will be rolled over, pending agreement on a debt reorganization. The objective is to give the debtor continuing access to a minimum of trade-related financing while negotiations take place and to prevent some banks from abruptly withdrawing their facilities at the expense of others.

Stock-of-debt operation. In the context of the Paris Club, an exit rescheduling of the eligible stock of debt (pre-cutoff date, non-ODA debt) for countries that have graduated from flow rescheduling. Stock operations on Cologne terms are given to countries that have reached their completion points under the enhanced HIPC Initiative.

Structural Adjustment Facility (SAF)/Enhanced Structural Adjustment Facility (ESAF). The Structural Adjustment Facility, established in 1986, and succeeded in 1987 by the Enhanced Structural Adjustment Facility, was until 1999 (when it was replaced by the PRGF) the concessional loan window of the IMF. ESAF was available to low-income member countries facing protracted balance of payments problems, and provided resources at an annual interest rate of 0.5 percent, and repayable over 10 years, including a grace period of 5½ years.

Subordination strategy. Policy of Paris Club creditors that loans extended after the cutoff date are not subject to rescheduling; therefore, pre-cutoff date loans are effectively subordinated to new lending.

Suppliers' credit. A financing arrangement under which an exporter extends credit to the buyer in the importing country.

Terms-of-reference rescheduling. Paris Club rescheduling involving only a small number of creditors. Typically this does not require a rescheduling meeting between the debtor country and its creditors, with the agreement being reached through an exchange of letters.

Tied-aid loans. Bilateral loans that are linked to purchases from the country providing the loans.

Toronto terms. See concessional rescheduling.

Transfer risk. The risk that a borrower will not be able to convert local currency into foreign exchange, and so will be unable to make debt service payments in foreign currency. The risk would usually arise from exchange restrictions imposed by the government in the borrower's country. This is a particular kind of political risk.

Uncovered claims. See claims payment.

Upper-middle-income countries. In the context of the Paris Club, countries not considered lower middle-income or low-income. These countries receive nonconcessional rescheduling terms—originally with flat repayment schedules, but in the 1990s increasingly with graduated payments schedules with usually up to 15 years' maturity and 8 years' grace period for commercial credits. ODA credits are rescheduled over 10 years, including 5–6 years' grace. In the context of the World Bank classification, upper-middle-income countries are those with a GNP per capita income in 2000 between $2,996–$9,265.

Table A8. Paris Club Reschedulings of Official Bilateral Debt: Amounts Consolidated in Successive Reschedulings, 1976–December 2000

(Millions of U.S. dollars)

Country/Agreement	I	II	III	IV	V	VI	VII	VIII	IX	X	XI	XII	XIII	Agreements Total Amount[1]	Number
Angola	446													446	1
Cambodia	249													249	1
Croatia	861													861	1
Djibouti	17													17	1
El Salvador	135													135	1
Gambia, The	17													17	1
Ghana	93[2]													93	1
Guatemala	440													440	1
Haiti	117													117	1
Pakistan	3,250													3,250	1
Rwanda	64													64	1
São Tomé and Príncipe	28													28	1
Vietnam	791													791	1
Algeria	5,345	7,320												12,665	2
Bosnia and Herzegovina	674	9												683	2
Chile	146	157												303	2
Dominican Republic	290	850												1,140	2
Egypt	6,350	27,864[3]												34,214	2
Ethiopia	441	184												625	2
Indonesia	4,176[3]	5,440												9,616	2
Kenya	535	302												837	2
Macedonia, FYR	288	46												334	2
Panama	19	200												219	2
Romania	234	736												970	2
Somalia	127	153												280	2
Trinidad and Tobago	209	110												319	2
Yemen	113	1,446												1,559	2
Albania	109	75	89											273	3
Bulgaria	640	251	200											1,091	3
Chad	24	24	12											60	3
Guinea-Bissau	25	21	195											241	3
Malawi	25	26	27											78	3
Mexico	1,199	1,912	2,400											5,511	3
Turkey	1,300	1,200	3,000											5,500	3
Brazil	2,337	4,178	4,992	10,500										22,007	4
Burkina Faso	71	36	64[4]	2										171	4
Congo, Republic of	756	1,052	1,175	1,758										4,741	4
Equatorial Guinea	38	10	32	51										131	4
Honduras	280	180	112	411										983	4
Liberia	35	25	17	17										94	4
Nicaragua	722	783	452	448										2,405	4
Nigeria	6,251	5,600	3,300	23,380										38,531	4
Sudan	487	203	518	249										1,457	4
Yugoslavia, Federal Republic of	500	812	901	1,291										3,504	4
Argentina	2,040	1,260	2,400	1,476	2,700									9,876	5
Benin	193	152	25	209[4]	5									584	5
Cameroon	535	1,080	1,259	1,129	1,350									5,353	5
Costa Rica	136	166	182	139	58									681	5
Guinea	196	123	203	156	123									801	5
Guyana	195	123	39	793[4]	240[5]									1,390	5
Jordan	587	771	1,147	400	821									3,726	5
Mali	63	44	20	33[4]	4									163	5
Philippines	757	862	1,850	1,096	—[6]									4,565	5
Russian Federation	14,363	7,100	6,400	40,200[3]	8,040									76,103	5
Morocco	1,152	1,124	1,008	969	1,390	1,303								6,946	6

Table A8 *(concluded)*

Country/Agreement	I	II	III	IV	V	VI	VII	VIII	IX	X	XI	XII	XIII	Agreements Total Amount[1]	Total Number
Peru	420	466	704	5,910	1,527	6,724[3]								15,751	6
Poland	2,110	10,930	1,400	9,027	10,400	29,871[3]								63,738	6
Tanzania	1,046	377	199	691	1,608	709								4,630	6
Bolivia	449	226	276	65	482	881[4]	561[5]							2,940	7
Central African Republic	72	13	14	28	4	32	23							186	7
Ecuador	142	450	438	397	339	293	804							2,863	7
Jamaica	105	62	124	147	179	127	291							1,035	7
Mauritania	68	27	90	52	218	66	98							619	7
Mozambique	283	361	719	440	664[7]	1,860[5]	71							4,398	7
Sierra Leone	39	37	25	86	164	42	39							432	7
Zambia	375	253	371	963	917	566	1,060							4,505	7
Côte d'Ivoire	230	213	370	567	934	806	1,849	1,332						6,301	8
Gabon	63	387	326	545	—[8]	1,360	1,030	687						4,398	8
Uganda	30	19	170	89	39	110[4]	148[5]	145[9]						750	8
Madagascar	140	107	89	128	212	254	139	1,247	57					2,373	9
Niger	36	26	38	34	37	48	116	160	128					623	9
Congo, Democratic Republic of	270	170	40	1,040	500	1,497	408	429	671	1,530				6,555	10
Togo	260	232	300	75	27	139	76	88	52	237				1,486	10
Senegal	75	74	72	122	65	79	143	107	114	237	169	590[4]	21	1,868	13
Total	66,684	88,441	37,784	105,113	33,047	46,767	6,856	4,195	1,022	2,004	169	590	21	392,690	307

Sources: Agreed Minutes of debt reschedulings; Paris Club Secretariat; and IMF staff estimates.

[1]Includes significant double-counting in cases where previously rescheduled debt has been rescheduled; also includes tranches that may not have been implemented.

[2]Limited terms of reference rescheduling of certain long-standing arrears.

[3]Total value of debt restructured.

[4]Stock-of-debt operation under Naples terms.

[5]Stock-of-debt operation under Lyon terms.

[6]The Philippines' 1994 rescheduling agreement was cancelled at the authorities' request.

[7]Coverage was broadened in 7/97.

[8]Gabon's 1991 rescheduling agreement was declared null and void.

[9]Stock-of-debt operation under Cologne terms.

Table A9. Rescheduling on Middle-Income Terms: Amounts Due and Consolidated Under Flow Rescheduling, August 1997–December 2000[1]

(Millions of U.S. dollars, unless otherwise indicated)

	Arrears[2]	Current Maturities[3]	Total
Debt service due	25,866	36,783	62,649
Pre-cutoff date debt	23,959	27,551	51,510
Not previously rescheduled	2,624	16,590	19,214
Previously rescheduled	21,334	10,961	32,295
Of which: Deferrals	341	164	504
Post-cutoff date debt	1,661	7,633	9,294
Short-term debt	247	1,599	1,846
Debt service treated	24,935	17,920	42,855
Consolidated amounts	22,374	17,090	39,464
Not previously rescheduled	1,179	12,134	13,313
Previously rescheduled[4]	21,195	4,956	26,151
Of which: Deferrals	341	164	504
Deferred for the first time	2,561	830	3,391
Post-cutoff date debt	1,196	795	1,991
Short-term debt	—	0	0
Moratorium interest	1,366	34	1,400
Debt service payable	2,620	20,152	22,771
Pre-cutoff date debt not treated[5]	1,585	10,461	12,046
Not previously rescheduled	1,445	4,456	5,901
Previously rescheduled	140	6,005	6,144
Of which: Deferrals	—	0	0
Post-cutoff date debt	465	6,838	7,303
Short-term debt	247	1,599	1,845
Moratorium interest	323	1,255	1,578
Debt service payable in percent of debt service due	10	55	36

Sources: Paris Club Secretariat and IMF staff estimates.

[1]Includes the reschedulings for: Djibouti I, Ecuador VII, Gabon VIII, Indonesia I, Indonesia II, Jordan V, Kenya II, Macedonia, FYR II, Nigeria IV, Pakistan I, and Russian Federation V.

[2]At the beginning of the consolidation period.

[3]Debt service falling due during the consolidation period.

[4]Including deferrals of debt treated under the most recent rescheduling agreement.

[5]Including late interest if not consolidated.

Table A10. Rescheduling on Low-Income Terms: Amounts Due and Consolidated Under Flow Rescheduling, August 1997–December 2000[1]

(Millions of U.S. dollars, unless otherwise indicated)

	Arrears[2]	Current Maturities[3]	Total
Debt service due	4,402	6,292	10,695
Pre-cutoff date debt	4,024	5,191	9,215
Not previously rescheduled	2,271	1,260	3,531
Previously rescheduled	1,753	3,931	5,684
Of which: Deferrals	189	396	584
Post-Cutoff date debt	331	1,058	1,389
Short-term debt	48	43	91
Debt service treated	3,698	5,014	8,712
Consolidated amounts	3,306	4,643	7,949
Not previously rescheduled	2,176	1,214	3,390
Previously rescheduled[4]	1,130	3,430	4,559
Of which: Deferrals	71	395	466
Deferred for the first time	392	371	763
Post-cutoff date debt	193	114	306
Short-term debt	9	19	28
Moratorium interest	71	82	153
Debt service payable	1,345	1,806	3,151
Pre-cutoff date debt not treated[5]	718	548	1,266
Not previously rescheduled	95	47	142
Previously rescheduled	623	501	1,124
Of which: Deferrals	118	1	119
Post-cutoff date debt	138	944	1,083
Short-term debt	39	24	63
Moratorium interest	569	447	1,016
Debt service payable in percent of debt service due	31	29	29

Sources: Paris Club Secretariat, and IMF staff estimates.

[1]Includes the reschedulings for: Albania II, Albania III, Benin V, Bosnia and Herzegovina I, Bosnia and Herzegovina I, Amendment, Burkina Faso IV, Cameroon V, Central African Republic VII, Côte d'Ivoire VIII, Honduras IV, Madagascar VIII, Amendments I and II, Mali V, Mauritania VII, Mozambique VI, Amendment, Nicaragua III, Nicaragua III, Amendment, Rwanda I, São Tomé and Príncipe I, Senegal XIII, Tanzania VI, Yemen II, and Zambia VII.

[2]At the beginning of the consolidation period.
[3]Debt service falling due during the consolidation period.
[4]Including deferrals of debt treated under the most recent rescheduling agreement.
[5]Including late interest if not consolidated.

Table A11. Amounts Restructured Under Stock-of-Debt Operations for Low-Income Countries on Naples Terms, August 1997–October 2000[1]

(Millions of U.S. dollars)

	Stocks Treated	Stocks Not Treated	Total Stocks
Total	581	529	1,109
Pre-cutoff date debt	581	177	758
Not previously rescheduled	15	0	16
Previously rescheduled	565	177	743
Nonconcessional	43	—	43
Toronto terms	321	—	321
London terms	202	43	245
Naples terms	—	134	134
Deferrals	—	—	—
Post-cutoff date debt	—	348	348
Short-term debt	—	3	3

Sources: Paris Club Secretariat, and IMF staff estimates.
[1]Rescheduling for Senegal XII.

Table A12. Amounts Restructured Under Stock-of-Debt Operations for Low-Income Countries on Lyon Terms, August 1997–December 2000[1]

(Millions of U.S. dollars)

	Stocks Treated	Stocks Not Treated	Total Stocks
Total	2,809	4,217	7,026
Pre-cutoff date debt	2,809	2,639	5,448
Not previously rescheduled	19	679	698
Previously rescheduled	2,790	1,960	4,750
Nonconcessional	399	—	399
Toronto terms	803	—	803
London terms	580	—	580
Naples terms	853	1,299	2,152
Lyon terms	73	651	723
Deferrals	83	10	93
Post-cutoff date debt	—	1,578	1,578
Short-term debt	—	1	1

Sources: Paris Club Secretariat, and IMF staff estimates.
[1]Includes the reschedulings for Bolivia VII, Guyana V, Mozambique VI, and Uganda VII.

Table A13. Amounts Restructured Under Stock-of-Debt Operations for Low-Income Countries on Cologne Terms, August 1997–December 2000[1]

(Millions of U.S. dollars)

	Stocks Treated	Stocks Not Treated	Total Stocks
Total	193	154	347
Pre-cutoff date debt	169	—	169
Not previously rescheduled	—	—	—
Previously rescheduled	169	—	169
Nonconcessional	—	—	—
Toronto terms	—	—	—
London terms	—	—	—
Naples terms	—	—	—
Lyon terms	169	—	169
Deferrals	—	—	—
Post-cutoff date debt	24	151	175
Short-term debt	—	3	3

Sources: Paris Club Secretariat, and IMF staff estimates.
[1]Rescheduling for Uganda VIII.

Table A14. Reschedulings and Deferrals of Official Bilateral Debt, 1976–2000

Debtor Countries	Number of Reschedulings[1]	Date of Agreement (M/D/Y)	Amount Consolidated[2] (Millions of U.S. dollars)	Consolidation Period[3] (Months)	Terms[4] Grace (Years)	Maturity (Years)
Albania	I TOR	12/01/93	109	. . .	2.8	7.3
Albania	II TOR	07/22/98	75	—	Naples terms[5]	
Albania	III TOR	10/14/99	89	15	1.1	5.6
Algeria	I	06/01/94	5,345	12	3.0	14.5[6]
Algeria	II	07/21/95	7,320	36	1.5	13.5[6]
Angola	I	07/20/89	446	15	6.0	9.5
Argentina	I	01/16/85	2,040	12	5.0	9.5
Argentina	II	05/20/87	1,260	14	4.9	9.5
Argentina	III	12/21/89	2,400	15	5.8	9.3
Argentina	IV	09/19/91	1,476	9	6.2	9.7
Argentina	V	07/22/92	2,700	29	1.1	13.6[6]
Benin	I	06/22/89	193	13	Toronto terms	
Benin	II	12/18/91	152	19	London terms	
Benin	III	06/21/93	25	29	London terms	
Benin	IV	10/25/96	209	Stock	Naples terms	
Benin	V	09/12/00	5	12	Cologne terms[7]	
Bolivia	I	06/25/86	449	12	5.0	9.5
Bolivia	II	11/14/88	226	15	5.9	9.3
Bolivia	III	03/15/90	276	24	Toronto terms	
Bolivia	IV	01/24/92	65	29	London terms	
Bolivia	V	03/24/95	482	36	Naples terms	
Bolivia	VI	12/14/95	881	Stock	Naples terms	
Bolivia	VII	10/30/98	561	Stock	Lyon terms	
Bosnia and Herzegovina	I	10/28/98	674	10	Naples terms	
Bosnia and Herzegovina	I Amended	07/28/00	9	12	Naples terms	
Brazil	I	11/23/83	2,337	17	4.0	7.5
Brazil	II	01/21/87	4,178	30	3.0	5.5
Brazil	III	07/28/88	4,992	20	5.0	9.5
Brazil	IV	02/26/92	10,500	20	1.8	13.3[6]
Bulgaria	I	04/17/91	640	12	6.5	10.0
Bulgaria	II	12/14/92	251	5	6.3	9.8
Bulgaria	III	04/13/94	200	13	5.9	9.4
Burkina Faso	I	03/15/91	71	15	Toronto terms	
Burkina Faso	II	05/07/93	36	33	London terms	
Burkina Faso	III	06/20/96	64	Stock	Naples terms	
Burkina Faso	IV	10/24/00	2	12	Cologne terms[7]	
Cambodia	I	01/26/95	249	30	Naples terms	
Cameroon	I	05/24/89	535	12	6.0	9.5
Cameroon	II	01/23/92	1,080	9	8.2	14.6
Cameroon	III	03/25/94	1,259	18	London terms	
Cameroon	IV	11/16/95	1,129	12	Naples terms[5]	
Cameroon	V	10/24/97	1,350	35	Naples terms[5]	
Central African Republic	I	06/12/81	72	12	4.0	8.5
Central African Republic	II	07/08/83	13	12	5.0	9.5
Central African Republic	III	11/22/85	14	18	4.8	9.3
Central African Republic	IV	12/14/88	28	18	Toronto terms	
Central African Republic	V	06/15/90	4	12	Toronto terms	
Central African Republic	VI	04/12/94	32	12	London terms	
Central African Republic	VII	09/25/98	23	34	Naples terms	
Chad	I TOR	10/24/89	24	15	Toronto terms	
Chad	II TOR	02/28/95	24	12	Naples terms	
Chad	III TOR	06/04/96	12	32	Naples terms	
Chile	I	07/17/85	146	18	2.8	6.3
Chile	II	04/02/87	157	21	2.6	6.1
Congo, Republic of	I	07/18/86	756	20	3.7	9.1
Congo, Republic of	II	09/13/90	1,052	21	5.8	14.3

Table A14 *(continued)*

Debtor Countries	Number of Reschedulings[1]	Date of Agreement (M/D/Y)	Amount Consolidated[2] (Millions of U.S. dollars)	Consolidation Period[3] (Months)	Terms[4] Grace (Years)	Terms[4] Maturity (Years)
Congo, Republic of	III	06/30/94	1,175	11	8.1	14.6
Congo, Republic of	IV	07/16/96	1,758	36	Naples terms	
Congo, Democratic Republic of	I	06/16/76	270	18	1.0	7.5
Congo, Democratic Republic of	II	07/07/77	170	12	3.0	8.5
Congo, Democratic Republic of	III	12/01/77	40	6	3.0	9.0
Congo, Democratic Republic of	IV	12/11/79	1,040	18	3.5	9.0
Congo, Democratic Republic of	V	07/09/81	500	12	4.0	9.5
Congo, Democratic Republic of	VI	12/20/83	1,497	12	5.0	10.5
Congo, Democratic Republic of	VII	09/18/85	408	15	4.9	9.4
Congo, Democratic Republic of	VIII	05/15/86	429	12	4.0	9.5
Congo, Democratic Republic of	IX	05/18/87	671	13	6.0	14.5
Congo, Democratic Republic of	X	06/23/89	1,530	13	Toronto terms	
Costa Rica	I	01/11/83	136	18	3.8	8.3
Costa Rica	II	04/22/85	166	15	4.9	9.4
Costa Rica	III	05/26/89	182	14	4.9	9.4
Costa Rica	IV	07/16/91	139	9	5.0	9.5
Costa Rica	V	06/22/93	58	—	2.0	6.5
Côte d'Ivoire	I	05/04/84	230	13	4.0	8.5
Côte d'Ivoire	II	06/25/85	213	12	4.0	8.5
Côte d'Ivoire	III	05/27/86	370	36	4.1	8.6
Côte d'Ivoire	IV	12/17/87	567	16	5.8	9.3
Côte d'Ivoire	V	12/18/89	934	16	7.8	13.3
Côte d'Ivoire	VI	11/20/91	806	12	8.0	14.5
Côte d'Ivoire	VII	03/22/94	1,849	37	London terms	
Côte d'Ivoire	VIII	04/24/98	1,332	36	Lyon terms	
Croatia	I	03/21/95	861	12	2.1	13.6
Djibouti	I TOR	03/22/00	17	32	4.5	9.0
Dominican Republic	I	05/21/85	290	15	4.9	9.4
Dominican Republic	II	11/22/91	850	18	7.8	14.3
Ecuador	I	07/28/83	142	12	3.0	7.5
Ecuador	II	04/24/85	450	36	3.0	7.5
Ecuador	III	01/20/88	438	14	4.9	9.4
Ecuador	IV	10/24/89	397	14	5.9	9.4
Ecuador	V	01/20/92	339	12	8.0	15.0
Ecuador	VI	06/27/94	293	6	8.3	14.8
Ecuador	VII	09/15/00	804	12	3.0	18.0
Egypt	I	05/22/87	6,350	18	4.7	9.2
Egypt	II	05/25/91	27,864[8]	Stock	2.5	35.0
El Salvador	I	09/17/90	135	13	8.0	14.5
Equatorial Guinea	I	07/22/85	38	18	4.5	9.0
Equatorial Guinea	II	03/03/89	10	. . .	Toronto terms	
Equatorial Guinea	III	04/02/92	32	12	London terms	
Equatorial Guinea	IV	12/15/94	51	21	London terms	
Ethiopia	I	12/16/92	441	35	London terms	
Ethiopia	II	01/24/97	184	34	Naples terms	
Gabon	I	06/20/78	63	—	. . .	. . .
Gabon	II	01/22/87	387	15	3.9	9.4
Gabon	III	03/21/88	326	12	5.0	9.5
Gabon	IV	09/19/89	545	16	4.0	10.0
Gabon	V	10/24/91[9]		15	5.0	10.0
Gabon	VI	04/15/94	1,360	12	2.0	14.5[6]
Gabon	VII	12/12/95	1,030	36	1.0	13.5[6]
Gabon	VIII	12/15/00	687	—	3.3	12.0
Gambia, The	I	09/19/86	17	12	5.0	9.5
Ghana	I TOR	04/07/96	93	—	1.0	5.0

Table A14 *(continued)*

Debtor Countries	Number of Reschedulings[1]	Date of Agreement (M/D/Y)	Amount Consolidated[2] (Millions of U.S. dollars)	Consolidation Period[3] (Months)	Terms[4]	
					Grace (Years)	Maturity (Years)
Guatemala	I	03/25/93	440	—	8.0	14.5
Guinea	I	04/18/86	196	14	4.9	9.4
Guinea	II	04/12/89	123	12	Toronto terms	
Guinea	III	11/18/92	203	12	London terms	
Guinea	IV	01/25/95	156	12	Naples terms[5]	
Guinea	V	02/26/97	123	36	Naples terms[5]	
Guinea-Bissau	I	10/27/87	25	18	9.7	19.2
Guinea-Bissau	II	10/26/89	21	15	Toronto terms	
Guinea-Bissau	III	02/23/95	195	36	Naples terms	
Guyana	I	05/23/89	195	14	9.9	19.4
Guyana	II	09/12/90	123	35	Toronto terms	
Guyana	III	05/06/93	39	17	London terms	
Guyana	IV	05/23/96	793	Stock	Naples terms	
Guyana	V	06/25/99	240	Stock	Lyon terms	
Haiti	I	05/30/95	117	13	Naples terms	
Honduras	I	09/14/90	280	11	8.1	14.6
Honduras	II	10/26/92	180	11	London terms	
Honduras	III	03/01/96	112	13	Naples terms[5]	
Honduras	IV	04/13/99	411	36	Naples terms	
Indonesia	I	09/23/98[10]	4,176	20	3.0	10.0[6]
Indonesia	II	04/13/00	5,440	24	3.2	15.0[6]
Jamaica	I	07/16/84	105	15	3.9	8.4
Jamaica	II	07/19/85	62	12	4.0	9.5
Jamaica	III	03/05/87	124	15	4.9	9.4
Jamaica	IV	10/24/88	147	18	4.7	9.2
Jamaica	V	04/26/90	179	18	4.8	9.3
Jamaica	VI	07/19/91	127	13	6.0	14.5
Jamaica	VII	01/25/93	291	36	5.0	13.5
Jordan	I	07/19/89	587	18	4.8	9.3
Jordan	II	02/28/92	771	18	7.7	14.3
Jordan	III	06/28/94	1,147	35	2.1	16.6[6]
Jordan	IV	05/23/97	400	21	3.0	17.5[6]
Jordan	V	05/20/99	821	37	3.0	18.0[6]
Kenya	I	01/19/94	535	—	1.3	7.8[6]
Kenya	II	11/15/00	302	12	3.0	20.0
Liberia	I	12/19/80	35	18	3.3	7.8
Liberia	II	12/16/81	25	18	4.1	8.6
Liberia	III	12/22/83	17	12	4.0	8.5
Liberia	IV	12/17/84	17	12	5.0	9.5
Macedonia, FYR	I	07/17/95	288	12	4.0	9.8
Macedonia, FYR	II TOR	09/01/00	46	12	1.0	5.5
Madagascar	I	04/30/81	140	18	3.8	8.3
Madagascar	II	07/13/82	107	12	3.8	8.3
Madagascar	III	03/23/84	89	18	4.8	10.3
Madagascar	IV	05/22/85	128	15	4.9	10.4
Madagascar	V	10/23/86	212	21	4.6	9.1
Madagascar	VI	10/28/88	254	21	Toronto terms	
Madagascar	VII	07/10/90	139	13	Toronto terms	
Madagascar	VIII	03/26/97	1,247	35	Naples terms	
Madagascar	VIII Amended 1	01/13/00	23	12	Naples terms	
Madagascar	VIII Amended 2	08/18/00	34	6	1.5	8.0
Malawi	I	09/22/82	25	12	3.5	8.0
Malawi	II	10/27/83	26	12	3.5	8.0
Malawi	III	04/22/88	27	14	9.9	19.4
Mali	I	10/27/88	63	16	Toronto terms	
Mali	II	11/22/89	44	26	Toronto terms	

Table A14 (continued)

Debtor Countries	Number of Reschedulings[1]	Date of Agreement (M/D/Y)	Amount Consolidated[2] (Millions of U.S. dollars)	Consolidation Period[3] (Months)	Terms[4]	
					Grace (Years)	Maturity (Years)
Mali	III	10/29/92	20	18	London terms	
Mali	IV	05/20/96	33	Stock	Naples terms	
Mali	V	10/24/00	4	10	Cologne terms[7]	
Mauritania	I	04/27/85	68	15	3.8	8.3
Mauritania	II	05/16/86	27	12	4.0	8.5
Mauritania	III	06/15/87	90	14	4.9	14.4
Mauritania	IV	06/19/89	52	12	Toronto terms	
Mauritania	V	01/26/93	218	24	London terms	
Mauritania	VI	06/28/95	66	36	Naples terms	
Mauritania	VII	03/16/00	98	36	Cologne terms	
Mexico	I	06/22/83	1,199	6	3.0	5.5
Mexico	II	09/17/86	1,912	15	4.0	8.5
Mexico	III	05/29/89	2,400	36	6.1	9.6
Morocco	I	10/25/83	1,152	16	3.8	7.3
Morocco	II	09/17/85	1,124	18	3.8	8.3
Morocco	III	03/06/87	1,008	16	4.7	9.2
Morocco	IV	10/26/88	969	18	4.7	9.2
Morocco	V	09/11/90	1,390	7	7.9	14.4
Morocco	VI	02/27/92	1,303	11	8.1	14.5
Mozambique	I	10/25/84	283	12	5.0	10.5
Mozambique	II	06/16/87	361	19	9.7	19.3
Mozambique	III	06/14/90	719	30	Toronto terms	
Mozambique	IV	03/23/93	440	24	London terms	
Mozambique	V	11/20/96	664	32	Lyon terms[11]	
Mozambique	VI	07/09/99	1,860	Stock	Lyon terms[12]	
Mozambique	VI Amended	03/15/00	71	12	0.2	4.7
Nicaragua	I	12/17/91	722	15	London terms	
Nicaragua	II	03/22/95	783	27	Naples terms	
Nicaragua	III	04/22/98	452	36	Naples terms	
Nicaragua	III Amended	03/16/99	448	27	1.6	6.1
Niger	I	11/14/83	36	12	4.5	8.5
Niger	II	11/30/84	26	14	4.9	9.4
Niger	III	11/21/85	38	12	5.1	9.5
Niger	IV	11/20/86	34	13	5.0	9.5
Niger	V	04/21/88	37	13	10.0	19.5
Niger	VI	12/16/88	48	12	Toronto terms	
Niger	VII	09/18/90	116	28	Toronto terms	
Niger	VIII	03/04/94	160	15	London terms	
Niger	IX	12/18/96	128	31	Naples terms	
Nigeria	I	12/16/86	6,251	15	4.9	9.4
Nigeria	II	03/02/89	5,600	16	4.8	9.3
Nigeria	III	01/18/91	3,300	15	7.9	14.3
Nigeria	IV	12/13/00	23,380	12	3.0	18.0
Pakistan	I	01/30/99[10]	3,250	24	3.0	18.0[6]
Panama	I	09/19/85	19	16	2.8	7.3
Panama	II	11/14/90	200	17	4.8	9.3
Peru	I	11/03/78	420	12	2.0	6.5
Peru	II	07/26/83	466	12	3.0	7.5
Peru	III	06/05/84	704	15	4.9	8.4
Peru	IV	09/17/91	5,910	15	7.9	14.5
Peru	V	05/04/93	1,527	39	6.9	13.4
Peru	VI	07/20/96	6,724	33	1.0	18.0
Philippines	I	12/20/84	757	18	4.8	9.3
Philippines	II	01/22/87	862	18	4.7	9.2
Philippines	III	05/27/89	1,850	25	5.5	9.0
Philippines	IV	06/20/91	1,096	14	7.9	14.4
Philippines	V	07/19/94[13]	. . .	17	7.9	14.4

Table A14 *(continued)*

Debtor Countries	Number of Reschedulings[1]	Date of Agreement (M/D/Y)	Amount Consolidated[2] (Millions of U.S. dollars)	Consolidation Period[3] (Months)	Terms[4]	
					Grace (Years)	Maturity (Years)
Poland	I	04/27/81	2,110	8	4.0	7.5
Poland	II	07/15/85	10,930	36	5.0	10.5
Poland	III	11/19/85	1,400	12	5.0	9.5
Poland	IV	10/30/87	9,027	12	4.5	9.0
Poland	V	02/16/90	10,400	15	8.3	13.8
Poland	VI	04/21/91	29,871[14]	Stock	6.5	18.0
Romania	I	07/28/82	234	12	3.0	6.0
Romania	II	05/18/83	736	12	3.0	6.0
Russian Federation	I	04/02/93[10]	14,363	12	5.0	9.5[6]
Russian Federation	II	06/02/94[10]	7,100	12	2.8	15.3[6]
Russian Federation	III	06/03/95[10]	6,400	12	2.8	15.3[6]
Russian Federation	IV	04/29/96[10]	40,200	39	4.1	22.7[6]
Russian Federation	V	08/01/99	8,040	18	1.4	20.0[6,15]
Rwanda	I	07/28/98	64	34	Naples terms	
São Tomé and Príncipe	I	05/16/00	28	37	Naples terms	
Senegal	I	10/12/81	75	12	4.0	8.5
Senegal	II	11/29/82	74	12	4.3	8.8
Senegal	III	12/21/83	72	12	4.0	8.5
Senegal	IV	01/18/85	122	18	3.8	8.3
Senegal	V	11/21/86	65	16	4.8	9.3
Senegal	VI	11/17/87	79	12	6.0	15.5
Senegal	VII	01/23/89	143	14	Toronto terms	
Senegal	VIII	02/12/90	107	12	Toronto terms	
Senegal	IX	06/21/91	114	12	Toronto terms	
Senegal	X	03/03/94	237	15	London terms	
Senegal	XI	04/20/95	169	29	Naples terms	
Senegal	XII	06/17/98	590	Stock	Naples terms	
Senegal	XIII	10/24/00	21	18	Cologne terms[7]	
Sierra Leone	I	09/15/77	39	24	1.5	8.5
Sierra Leone	II	02/08/80	37	16	4.2	9.7
Sierra Leone	III	02/08/84	25	12	5.0	10.0
Sierra Leone	IV	11/19/86	86	18	4.8	9.2
Sierra Leone	V	11/20/92	164	30	London terms	
Sierra Leone	VI	07/20/94	42	17	London terms	
Sierra Leone	VII	03/28/96	39	24	Naples terms	
Somalia	I	03/06/85	127	12	5.0	9.5
Somalia	II	07/22/87	153	24	9.5	19.0
Sudan	I	11/13/79	487	21	3.0	9.5
Sudan	II	03/18/82	203	18	4.5	9.5
Sudan	III	02/04/83	518	12	5.5	15.0
Sudan	IV	05/03/84	249	12	6.0	15.5
Tanzania	I	09/18/86	1,046	12	5.0	9.5
Tanzania	II	12/13/88	377	6	Toronto terms	
Tanzania	III	03/16/90	199	12	Toronto terms	
Tanzania	IV	01/21/92	691	30	London terms	
Tanzania	V	01/21/97	1,608	36	Naples terms	
Tanzania	VI	04/13/00	709	36	Cologne terms	
Togo	I	06/15/79	260	21	2.8	8.3
Togo	II	02/20/81	232	24	4.0	8.5
Togo	III	04/12/83	300	12	5.0	9.5
Togo	IV	06/06/84	75	16	4.8	9.3
Togo	V	06/24/85	27	12	5.0	10.5
Togo	VI	03/22/88	139	15	7.9	15.3
Togo	VII	06/20/89	76	14	Toronto terms	
Togo	VIII	07/09/90	88	24	Toronto terms	
Togo	IX	06/19/92	52	9	London terms	
Togo	X	02/23/95	237	33	Naples terms	

Table A14 *(concluded)*

Debtor Countries	Number of Reschedulings[1]	Date of Agreement (M/D/Y)	Amount Consolidated[2] (Millions of U.S. dollars)	Consolidation Period[3] (Months)	Terms[4] Grace (Years)	Maturity (Years)
Trinidad and Tobago	I	01/25/89	209	14	4.9	9.4
Trinidad and Tobago	II	04/27/90	110	13	5.0	9.5
Turkey	I	05/20/78	1,300	13	2.0	6.5
Turkey	II	07/25/79	1,200	12	3.0	7.5
Turkey	III	07/23/80	3,000	36	4.5	9.0
Uganda	I	11/18/81	30	12	4.5	9.0
Uganda	II	12/01/82	19	12	6.5	8.0
Uganda	III	06/19/87	170	12	6.0	14.5
Uganda	IV	01/26/89	89	18	Toronto terms	
Uganda	V	06/17/92	39	24	London terms	
Uganda	VI	02/20/95	110	Stock	Naples terms	
Uganda	VII	04/24/98	148	Stock	Lyon terms	
Uganda	VIII	09/12/00	145	Stock	Cologne terms	
Vietnam	I	12/14/93	791	—	London terms	
Yemen, Republic of	I	09/24/96	113	10	Naples terms	
Yemen, Republic of	II	11/20/97	1,446	36	Naples terms	
Yugoslavia[16]	I	05/22/84	500	12	4.0	6.5
Yugoslavia[16]	II	05/24/85	812	16	3.8	8.3
Yugoslavia[16]	III	05/13/86	901	12	3.9	9.4
Yugoslavia[16]	IV	07/13/88	1,291	15	5.9	9.4
Zambia	I	05/16/83	375	12	5.0	9.5
Zambia	II	07/20/84	253	12	5.0	9.5
Zambia	III	03/04/86	371	12	5.0	9.5
Zambia	IV	07/12/90	963	18	Toronto terms	
Zambia	V	07/23/92	917	33	London terms	
Zambia	VI	02/28/96	566	36	Naples terms	
Zambia	VII	04/16/99	1,060	36	Naples terms	

Sources: Paris Club, and IMF staff estimates.

[1]Roman numerals indicate, for each country, the number of debt reschedulings, in the period beginning 1976. For terms of reference reschedulings (TOR), date of informal meeting of creditors on the terms to be applied in the bilateral reschedulings.

[2]Includes debt service formally rescheduled as well as postponed maturities.

[3]In a number of cases consolidation period was extended subsequently.

[4]Terms for current maturities due on medium- and long-term debt covered by the rescheduling agreement and not rescheduled previously. Grace and maturity are calculated from the middle of the consolidation period plus 6 months.

[5]Naples terms with a 50 percent NPV reduction.

[6]Graduated payments schedule.

[7]The existing Paris Club agreement was topped up to Cologne terms.

[8]Total value of debt restructured for Egypt in 1991 includes the cancellation of military debt by the United States.

[9]Gabon's 1991 rescheduling agreement was declared null and void.

[10]Creditors met under the chairmanship of the Group of Participating Creditor Countries or as Group of Official Bilateral Creditors.

[11]Initial rescheduling was on Naples terms. It was topped up in January 1998 to Lyon terms retroactively from July 1997.

[12]With 90 percent debt reduction.

[13]The 1994 rescheduling was canceled at the request of the authorities.

[14]Total value of debt restructured for Poland in 1991.

[15]20-year maturity for debt not previously rescheduled.

[16]Former Socialist Federal Republic of Yugoslavia.

BIBLIOGRAPHY

Andrews, David, Anthony R. Boote, Syed S. Rizavi, and Sukhwinder Singh, 1999, *Debt Relief for Low-Income Countries*, IMF Pamphlet Series No. 51, revised (Washington: International Monetary Fund).

Boote, Anthony R., and Kamau Thugge, 1999, *Debt Relief for Low-Income Countries: The HIPC Initiative*, IMF Pamphlet Series No. 51 (Washington: International Monetary Fund).

Boote, Anthony R., Doris C. Ross, Mariano Cortes, Christina Daseking, Vitali Kramarenko, Toshiro Nishizawa, Saqib Rizavi, and Kevin Ross, 1998, *Official Financing for Developing Countries*, World Economic and Financial Surveys (Washington: International Monetary Fund).

Daseking, Christina and Robert Powell, 1999, *From Toronto Terms to the HIPC Initiative: A Brief History of Debt Relief for Low Income Countries*, IMF Working Paper 142 (Washington: International Monetary Fund).

Collier, Paul and David Dollar, 1999, *Aid Allocation and Poverty Reduction* (Washington: International Monetary Fund).

Feyzioglu, Tashar, Viraya Swaroop, and Min Zhu, 1998, *A Panel Data Analysis of the Fungibility of Foreign Aid*, World Bank Economic Review No. 12, January (Washington: World Bank).

Kuhn, Michael G., Balazs Horvath, and Christopher J. Jarvis, 1995, *Officially Supported Export Credits: Recent Developments and Prospects*, World Economic and Financial Surveys (Washington: International Monetary Fund).

Lensink, Robert, and Oliver Morrisey, 1999, *Uncertainty of Aid Inflows and the Aid-Growth Relationship*, CREDIT Research Paper No. 99/3 (University of Nothingham).

Organization for Economic Cooperation and Development, Development Assistance Committee, 1996, *Shaping the 21st Century: The Contribution of Development Cooperation* (Washington).

———, 1998, *Strengthening Development Partnerships: A Working Checklist* (Paris).

Powel, Robert, 2000, *Debt Relief for Poor Countries*, Finance and Development, Vol. 37, No. 4 (Washington: International Monetary Fund).

Stephens, Malcolm, 1999, *The Changing Role of Export Credit Agencies* (Washington: International Monetary Fund).

World Bank, 1998, *Assessing Aid: What Works, What Doesn't, and Why* (Washington: Oxford University Press).

World Economic and Financial Surveys

This series (ISSN 0258-7440) contains biannual, annual, and periodic studies covering monetary and financial issues of importance to the global economy. The core elements of the series are the *World Economic Outlook* report, usually published in May and October, and the annual report on *International Capital Markets*. Other studies assess international trade policy, private market and official financing for developing countries, exchange and payments systems, export credit policies, and issues discussed in the *World Economic Outlook*. Please consult the IMF *Publications Catalog* for a complete listing of currently available World Economic and Financial Surveys.

World Economic Outlook: A Survey by the Staff of the International Monetary Fund

The *World Economic Outlook*, published twice a year in English, French, Spanish, and Arabic, presents IMF staff economists' analyses of global economic developments during the near and medium term. Chapters give an overview of the world economy; consider issues affecting industrial countries, developing countries, and economies in transition to the market; and address topics of pressing current interest.
ISSN 0256-6877.
$42.00 (academic rate: $35.00); paper.

2001. (May). ISBN 1-58906-032-6. **Stock #WEO EA 0012001.**
2000. (Oct.). ISBN 1-55775-975-8. **Stock #WEO EA 0022000.**
2000. (May). ISBN 1-55775-936-7. **Stock #WEO EA 012000.**
1999. (Oct.). ISBN 1-55775-839-5. **Stock #WEO EA 299.**
1999. (May). ISBN 1-55775-809-3. **Stock #WEO-199.**

Official Financing for Developing Countries
by a staff team in the IMF's Policy Development and Review Department led by Doris C. Ross and Richard T. Harmsen

This study provides information on official financing for developing countries, with the focus on low-income countries. It updates the 1998 edition and reviews developments in direct financing by official and multilateral sources.
$42.00 (academic rate: $35.00); paper.

1998. ISBN 1-55775-702-X. **Stock #WEO-1397.**
1995. ISBN 1-55775-527-2. **Stock #WEO-1395.**

Exchange Rate Arrangements and Currency Convertibility: Developments and Issues
by a staff team led by R. Barry Johnston

A principal force driving the growth in international trade and investment has been the liberalization of financial transactions, including the liberalization of trade and exchange controls. This study reviews the developments and issues in the exchange arrangements and currency convertibility of IMF members.
$20.00 (academic rate: $12.00); paper.

1999. ISBN 1-55775-795-X. **Stock #WEO EA 0191999.**

World Economic Outlook Supporting Studies
by the IMF's Research Department

These studies, supporting analyses and scenarios of the *World Economic Outlook*, provide a detailed examination of theory and evidence on major issues currently affecting the global economy.
$25.00 (academic rate: $20.00); paper.
2000. ISBN 1-55775-893-X. **Stock #WEO EA 0032000.**

International Capital Markets: Developments, Prospects, and Key Policy Issues
by a staff team led by Donald J. Mathieson and Garry J. Schinasi

This year's *International Capital Markets* report assesses recent developments in mature and emerging financial markets and analyzes key systemic issues affecting global financial markets. The report discusses the main risks in the period ahead; identifies sources of, and possible measures to avoid, instability in OTC derivatives markets; reviews initiatives to "involve" the private sector in preventing and resolving crises, and discusses the role of foreign-owned banks in emerging markets.
$42.00 (academic rate: $35.00); paper
2000. (Sep.). ISBN 1-55775-949-9. **Stock #WEO EA 0062000.**
1999. (Sep.). ISBN 1-55775-852-2. **Stock #WEO EA 699.**
1998. (Sep.). ISBN 1-55775-770-4. **Stock #WEO-698.**

Toward a Framework for Financial Stability
by a staff team led by David Folkerts-Landau and Carl-Johan Lindgren

This study outlines the broad principles and characteristics of stable and sound financial systems, to facilitate IMF surveillance over banking sector issues of macroeconomic significance and to contribute to the general international effort to reduce the likelihood and diminish the intensity of future financial sector crises.
$25.00 (academic rate: $20.00); paper.
1998. ISBN 1-55775-706-2. **Stock #WEO-016.**

Trade Liberalization in IMF-Supported Programs
by a staff team led by Robert Sharer

This study assesses trade liberalization in programs supported by the IMF by reviewing multiyear arrangements in the 1990s and six detailed case studies. It also discusses the main economic factors affecting trade policy targets.
$25.00 (academic rate: $20.00); paper.
1998. ISBN 1-55775-707-0. **Stock #WEO-1897.**

Private Market Financing for Developing Countries
by a staff team from the IMF's Policy Development and Review Department led by Steven Dunaway

This study surveys recent trends in flows to developing countries through banking and securities markets. It also analyzes the institutional and regulatory framework for developing country finance; institutional investor behavior and pricing of developing country stocks; and progress in commercial bank debt restructuring in low-income countries.
$20.00 (academic rate: $12.00); paper.
1995. ISBN 1-55775-526-4. **Stock #WEO-1595.**

Available by series subscription or single title (including back issues); academic rate available only to full-time university faculty and students. For earlier editions please inquire about prices.

The IMF *Catalog of Publications* is available on-line at the Internet address listed below.

Please send orders and inquiries to:
International Monetary Fund, Publication Services, 700 19th Street, N.W.
Washington, D.C. 20431, U.S.A.
Tel.: (202) 623-7430   Telefax: (202) 623-7201
E-mail: publications@imf.org
Internet: http://www.imf.org